INDIAN
Vegetarian *feast*

ANJUM ANAND

Photography by Emma Lee

STERLING EPICURE
New York

To Adi and Mahi, with
all my love ... always.

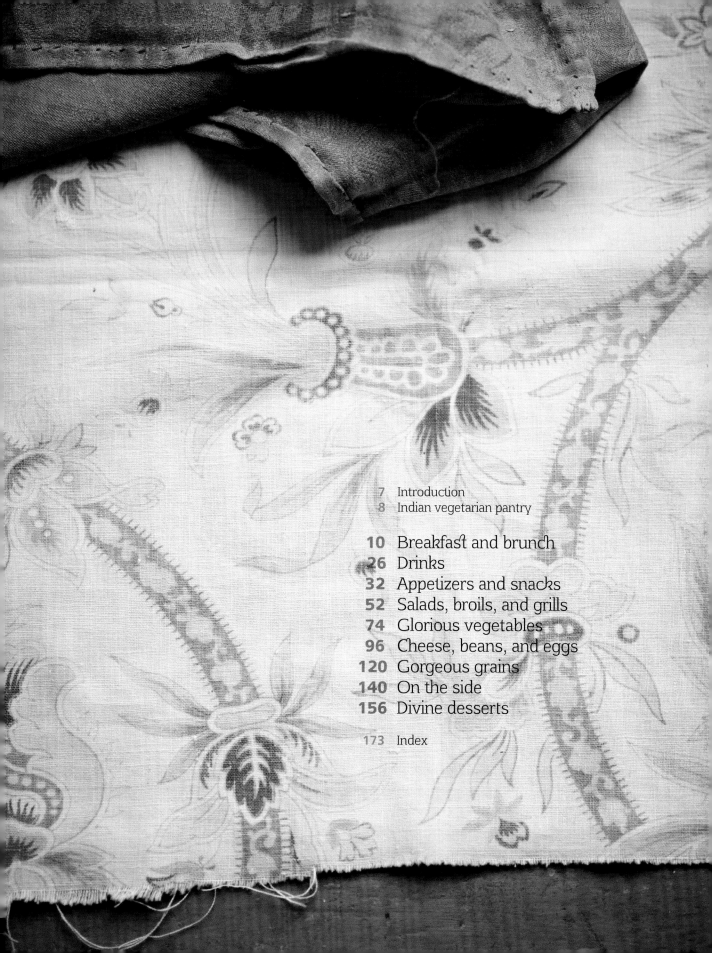

I was raised by a vegetarian mother. She had an arranged marriage, which makes you think she would have been introduced to a "suitable" partner, but really my father couldn't have been more different from her when it came to food. His tastes were as gourmand as hers were restrained. He tells colorful stories about fishing with his brothers, taking their prize catch home, and making a big pot of curry, but food never features in my mother's childhood tales. Once married, however, she started to cook the rich, meaty curries my father loved, and served them up as well as her simple but equally tasty vegetable and lentil dishes. I was brought up eating both.

In a funny twist of fate, I then married a vegetarian who comes from generations of vegetarians. So my children are vegetarian. As I have been married for nine years—and my husband doesn't cook —that's a lot of vegetarian meals. Like my mother, I have learned a new way to cook, creating new dishes, and tinkering with flavors to keep my family well fed and enjoying their meals.

Luckily, my culinary heritage is replete with amazing vegetarian dishes, as two-thirds of India has followed a meat-free diet for thousands of years, either because the people can't afford meat on a regular basis, or because they believe that eating it is bad for the soul (in a country that believes in reincarnation, they aren't taking any chances). Either way, this has given them a lot of time to perfect the culinary uses of lentils, beans, and dairy products into a vast spectrum of dishes. I have always said my desert island ingredient would be the humble Bengal gram (chana dal), a type of lentil. It can be made into a curry, stir-fried with spices into a protein-rich side dish, even used to make a dessert. It is also ground into flour and then made into bread, or batter for spiced pancakes or bhajis, or spiced and steamed savory lentil cakes. Indians are alchemists of the vegetarian table, and can conjure thousands of uses from their beans or dairy products.

The recipes in this book have their feet firmly planted in India's amazing regional food, but also contain influences from my life and travels. Many of the dishes here are Indian classics, others are refreshed and revised meals that I love. There are also a few which are just hanging by a homespun cotton thread to an Indian heritage, but are too delicious not to be included.

I have enjoyed writing this book more than any other; I've cooked with foods I hadn't tried before and experimented with new flavor combinations. I find the world of meat-free living bountiful, beautiful, and a feast for so many of the senses. I hope you enjoy the food as much as I do.

Anjum

Indian vegetarian pantry

Most of the ingredients necessary to whip up exciting, nourishing vegetarian food can be kept handy in your pantry. As long as you have the very basic fresh ingredients—such as onions, gingerroot, garlic, tomatoes, and yogurt—you should be able to whip up delicious meals without last-minute dashes to the stores. This is a really comprehensive list, so don't feel that you need to buy and store all of these in your kitchen, but do have a look through and see which make you feel hungry! The more varied your vegetarian diet the better, so be adventurous and seek out ingredients that you don't eat ... yet.

BEANS

Obviously, these are a great source of protein, as well as key minerals. I store both dried and canned beans. I prefer the texture and flavor of dried beans, which need to be soaked overnight before cooking, but I also have cans of those beans I eat often, just in case of sudden cravings. I never buy canned lentils, as these do not need soaking. There are a whole panoply of lentils and they are your friends in the kitchen: they need little attention and minimal fuss to fashion into beautiful curries. Here are some of the bean and lentil varieties I use most often.

BEANS	LENTILS
Black-eyed peas	Bengal gram *(chana dal)*
Cannellini beans	Black gram *(urad dal)*
Chickpeas	Puy lentils
Kidney beans	Red lentils *(masoor dal)*
Lima beans	Split black gram *(dhuli hui ma dal)*
	Split pigeon peas *(toor dal)*
	Yellow lentils *(mung dal)*

SPICES

Essential to the Indian diet; Indians are the alchemists of the spice rack. I recommend you increase your spice larder by one jar or package a week, as these will really add a wow factor to your daily diet.

WHOLE	GROUND
Ajowan seeds	Asafetida
Black cardamom pods	Chaat masala
Black peppercorns	*(a store-bought blend of tangy*
Brown mustard seeds	*spices, this is really useful)*
Cassia bark *(a hardier, less*	Chili powder
sweet version of cinnamon)	Dried fenugreek leaves
Cloves	*(a great savory flavor)*
Coriander seeds	Dried mint
Cumin seeds	*(adds lovely fragrance)*
Curry leaves *(ideally fresh;*	Mango powder
if dried or frozen, use with	*(gives a welcome sour note)*
a heavier hand)	Pomegranate powder *(with*
Dried red chiles	*an unusual, delicious tang)*
Fennel seeds	Turmeric
Fenugreek seeds	
Green cardamom pods	
Mace	
Nutmeg	
Panch phoran	
(a mix of five seeds)	

How to roast spices

Only roast whole spices. Place the spices in a moderately hot, dry skillet and toast over gentle heat. Shake the skillet often so the spices brown evenly. (Do not use nonstick skillets as the coating may smoke and this is thought to be toxic.) As the spices roast, they color and become aromatic. Take them off the heat once they turn a few shades darker. (For the already dark spices, test by aroma instead.) Remove them from the skillet or they will continue to brown and might burn. Roasted spices can be ground in a mortar and pestle, or a spice or coffee grinder kept for the purpose.

GRAINS

These don't have to be dull, in fact these days they are positively fashionable! Some can add protein to the diet.

Basmati rice, white and brown.
I use a lot of brown at home for family food.
Beaten rice (poha).
This is cooked rice that has been dried, then flattened into a flake. It is fluffy and delicious and often made into a pilaf. Don't confuse this with the flaked raw rice that you can buy in some supermarkets.
Bulgur wheat, nutty and delicious.
Chapati flour (atta), made from whole wheat berries.
Gram flour (besan), made from chickpeas.
This has a lovely flavor and is high in protein.
Quinoa, another high-protein grain that is really good as part of a vegetarian diet.
Semolina, a lovely, couscous-like grain that can be used in a batter to add crunch, or in a pilaf or dessert.

NUTS AND SEEDS

Nuts feature heavily in Indian food, giving texture or flavor, or working as thickening agents. I have also included in this book chia seeds, which are believed by many to be very healthy, especially good for vegetarians, and, once softened in liquid, have an interesting gelatinous texture. I have used them in this book in my kulfi recipe, but I often add some to my oatmeal or yogurt.

Almonds	Peanuts, roasted or raw
Cashews	Pistachios, roasted or raw
Coconut: milk, cream, dry unsweetened, and frozen and grated	Poppy seeds
	Sesame seeds

How to make paneer

Paneer is an unsalted, crumbly white Indian cheese, which is really easy to make.
Bring 8 cups of whole milk to a boil in a heavy-bottom pan; stir and scrape the bottom often to ensure the milk does not burn. Boil for five minutes, then add generous 1 cup live yogurt or the juice of 1 lemon (yogurt gives a softer paneer). Stir while it splits into curds and whey. Line a colander with a cheesecloth (or other clean cloth) and pour in the contents of the pan. Rinse with cold water. Tie the cloth into a sack, then tie this to the kitchen faucet and let drain for 20 minutes. Next, place it on a thick board, still enclosed, and pat it out so it forms a 1-inch-thick disk. Place a large weight on top (I use a pan filled with water) and put the board in the sink. The water will seep out. Leave until it solidifies; this will take 1 to 2 hours, more for a solid paneer, less for a softer texture. This recipe yields 9 ounces of paneer. Keep, stored in water, in the refrigerator. Before cooking, soak in hot water for five to 10 minutes to soften.

NOTES ON...

...GINGERROOT In many recipes I read, ginger is measured by length, but I find this an unreliable way to measure the rhizome, as the thickness can vary so much. I measure it in ounces, or sometimes teaspoons, to get just the right amount of ginger flavor every time.

...CHILI The heat varies from batch to batch, and this extends to chili powder, so always add sparingly. You can always add extra chili powder at the end of cooking for more heat, if you want it.

...DOUBLING RECIPES As a general rule you can double all the recipes in this book, but you have to be careful about the amount of spices you use. Only add another 50 percent of the whole spices used, to double a recipe. (The exception to this rule is cumin seeds; you should double the amount of these.)

BREAKFAST
AND BRUNCH

A lovely weekend breakfast dish; easy but really special. Brioche is the best bread to use in my opinion, as the resulting toast is both buttery and soft on the inside and lightly crisp on the outside, but your everyday loaf of bread would be just fine, too. Dry unsweetened coconut is one of my pantry staples and here it adds a lovely texture as well as its sun-drenched, coastal flavor. If I am making this for guests at a weekend brunch, I add fresh seasonal soft fruit on the side as well as a little Greek yogurt and a handful of Jaggery Caramelized Walnuts (see below).

Coconut French toast

Whisk together the eggs, milk, and sugar. Spread the dry unsweetened coconut on a small plate.

Heat the oil and butter in a large nonstick skillet over medium heat. Dip one slice of bread in the batter for about 30 to 40 seconds, pressing lightly to help the bread absorb the custard. Transfer to the plate of dry unsweetend coconut and press gently, turning to coat both sides. Place straight in the hot pan, then repeat with the other slices.

Cook over moderate heat for about two minutes, or until golden, then carefully flip and brown the other side. Serve hot from the pan, or keep warm while you cook the rest. Offer maple syrup on the table for those who want extra sweetness.

SERVES 4

2 large eggs
generous ¾ cup whole milk
3 tablespoons sugar (use only 2 tablespoons
  if you are going to serve these with syrup)
6 good tablespoons dry unsweetened coconut
2 tablespoons vegetable oil
couple of little pieces of unsalted butter
4 slices of brioche, or everyday bread
natural maple syrup, to serve (optional)

Jaggery caramelized walnuts
MAKES A SMALL BATCH

I love these scattered over sweet breakfasts, or they make a great snack when I want something sweet but healthy. Jaggery is a completely unrefined sugar, sold in blocks, and renowned for its healthy properties. It is full of iron and other minerals and believed to keep your lungs clean. The best quality is dark and hard, but larger supermarkets sell a softer jaggery which also works here.

  Take 3 ounces of jaggery and chop or pound it into smallish pieces. Place in a skillet and cook over medium-low heat, stirring often, until it melts and starts to get more glassy and less cloudy; this only takes a few minutes. Stir in generous ¾ cup of walnuts, stir to coat well, and cook for another minute. Pour out onto a sheet of baking parchment, or an oiled plate, and separate the walnuts. You have to work quickly as the jaggery will start to harden. (If so, return to the pan and heat a little to melt it again.) Let cool and harden. Store in an airtight container.

Bananas are one of Kerala's most prolific fruits and are used in everything. In Kerala at breakfast time, they might be simply sliced on top of rice pancakes, or steamed in batter in a banana leaf, or mixed with grated coconut and cashews and used to fill a pancake. My own version definitely uses western artistic license, as the bananas are mashed into a quick and easy American-inspired fluffy pancake. I add cumin seeds to the batter, but you can leave them out if you prefer.

Keralan-inspired banana pancakes with peanut butter

Heat the rounded tablespoon of butter in a small pan over gentle heat until it is lightly browned and smells nutty, then set aside.

Mix together the flour, salt, sugar, baking powder, and cumin seeds. In a separate bowl, mash the two bananas with a fork until they have completely broken down, then whisk in the eggs, followed by the milk and melted butter. Make a well in the dry ingredients, pour in the wet ones, and whisk, drawing in the sides until you have a smooth batter.

Heat a teaspoon of butter in your pan (I use a cast-iron pancake pan, but a skillet will work). Add scant ¼ cup of the batter for each pancake and cook over moderate heat until bubbles start to appear on the surface and the base is lightly golden. Flip over and cook the other side until lightly golden as well. Keep the pancakes warm while you cook the rest.

For each serving, place two pancakes on a plate, sandwiching a few slices of banana in the middle, scoop a tablespoon of peanut butter on top, and drizzle with the syrup.

MAKES 8 LARGE-ISH PANCAKES

1 rounded tablespoon unsalted butter, plus more to cook
scant 1½ cups all-purpose flour, sifted
good pinch of salt
3 tablespoons superfine sugar
1½ teaspoons baking powder
good pinch of cumin seeds
2 large, ripe bananas
2 large eggs
1¼ cups whole milk

TO SERVE
1 ripe banana, cut on the diagonal into thin slices
4 rounded tablespoons unsweetened chunky peanut butter
natural maple syrup

I know this isn't Indian in origin, but it is so delicious I couldn't resist putting it in the book. I made this compote to go with my kulfi (see page 169), but it was even more divine eaten for breakfast the next morning. Granola is so easy to make that, once you've done it, you will never buy it again. Here it adds a lovely crunch. I like it with pistachios, almonds, cashews, pumpkin and sunflower seeds, but use your own favorite nuts and seeds. I haven't added dried fruit to it as there is some in the compote, but you can add raisins, dried cherries, dried blueberries, or any other you like, with the coconut.

Blackberry-violet compote and easy granola

To make the granola, preheat the oven to 275°F. Mix the oats, nuts and seeds, cinnamon, and salt in a cookie sheet. Make a well in the middle, pour in all the wet ingredients, and mix well. Bake for 40 minutes, stirring every eight to nine minutes. Add the coconut when there are five minutes to go. Take out of the oven once golden; it will crisp up as it cools. Once cold, store in an airtight container.

Place the blackberries in a pan with a good splash of water and heat until they start to soften. Add the syrup and dried fruit and cook for another minute, then take off the heat. Add another splash of water if the fruit looks a little dry. Taste and balance the flavors, adding more syrup or a squeeze of orange juice to balance the sweetness.
Serve the compote hot or cold with Greek yogurt and the granola.

MAKES ENOUGH FOR 4

FOR THE GRANOLA
generous 1¾ cups old-fashioned rolled oats
½ cup mixed nuts and seeds
½ teaspoon ground cinnamon
good pinch of salt
¾ teaspoon vanilla extract
1½ tablespoons vegetable oil
scant ¼–¼ cup natural maple syrup
1½ tablespoons honey
¼ cup coconut flakes or dry unsweetened
   coconut

FOR THE REST
2¾ cups blackberries, washed
4–5 tablespoons violet syrup, or to taste
large handful of dried blueberries or raisins
squeeze of orange juice (if needed)
Greek yogurt, to serve

These are known as chillas and are a high-protein, gluten-free savory pancake. They are eaten as they are, with spicy ketchup or chutney (see below), for breakfast or as a snack. Very quick to make, the pancakes are nutritious and filling, so are popular in vegetarian Indian homes. I also love them for an easy lunch with some simple vegetables on the side.

Spicy, crisp chickpea pancakes

Whisk ½–scant ⅔ cup of water into the gram flour, making sure there are no lumps. Add all the remaining ingredients except the oil and mix well. Taste for seasoning and adjust if necessary. The batter should have the consistency of heavy cream.

Heat around ½–¾ teaspoon of the oil in a cast-iron griddle pan and pour in one-quarter of the batter, to make a pancake about 6 inches in diameter. Cook for one to two minutes, or until lightly golden on the base, then drizzle another ½–¾ teaspoon of oil over the top and flip the pancake over. Cook, pressing down to help the edges crisp up. Once the base is golden, take out and repeat with the remaining oil and batter.

Serve hot, with spicy ketchup or Coastal Coconut Chutney (see below).

MAKES 4 PANCAKES

generous 1 cup gram (chickpea) flour
½ teaspoon cumin seeds
¼ teaspoon ajowan seeds
1½ teaspoons peeled and grated gingerroot
2 garlic cloves, peeled and grated
salt, to taste
¼ teaspoon turmeric
2 tablespoons chopped cilantro leaves
½ onion, minced
1 small tomato, chopped
2 teaspoons lemon juice
1–2 tablespoons vegetable oil

Coastal coconut chutney
MAKES ³/₄ CUP

A really lovely chutney from the South, this adds texture, creaminess and heat.

Place generous 1 cup grated coconut, 1–2 green chiles, ¼ ounce peeled gingerroot, a pinch of salt, and scant ½ cup creamy Greek yogurt in a blender. Dry roast 1½ tablespoons Bengal gram (chana dal) until colored all over, then tip into the blender with 1 tablespoon lemon juice. Blend until smooth, adding water to help. Heat 1 teaspoon vegetable oil in a pan, then add ⅔ teaspoon mustard seeds. When the popping dies down, add 8 curry leaves and cook for 10 seconds longer. Pour this into the chutney and stir it all together. Taste, adjust the seasoning and lemon juice, then serve

Kedgeree is such a British institution that I felt some trepidation in giving it my own Indian twist ... the irony of this does not escape me! But I did. This is a creamy version, based on a South Indian breakfast dish. It is nutritious and filling but not heavy.

Creamy kedgeree

Place the rice and lentils in a pan and wash them well. Drain, add the milk and 3½ cups of water, and bring to a boil. Reduce the heat and simmer, partially covered, until just cooked (around 10 minutes).

Meanwhile, heat 4 tablespoons of the ghee or butter in a separate pan and add the cumin seeds. Once they darken, add the onion and cook until turning golden brown. Add the garlic and ginger and cook gently until the garlic just starts to color. Stir in the ground spices and salt and cook for another minute. Pour in a splash of water.

By now the lentils and rice should be cooked. Stir in the spiced onions and cook for another few minutes. Add the lemon juice, herbs, and cashews, taste, and adjust the seasoning and consistency; it should be thick and creamy but not loose, so add a little water, or boil off extra over high heat, as necessary. Cover as you fry your eggs.

Heat the remaining ghee or butter in a nonstick skillet. Crack in the eggs and sizzle until the whites are cooked and the yolks still soft (I like crispy edges, too). Sprinkle over a little salt, pepper, and chili powder. Mound the rice on warm plates, top with the eggs, and serve.

SERVES 4

1 cup basmati rice
½ cup yellow lentils (mung dal)
generous 2 cups whole milk
6 tablespoons ghee or unsalted butter
1 teaspoon cumin seeds
1 large onion, chopped
4 garlic cloves, peeled and minced
1 tablespoon peeled and minced gingerroot
½ teaspoon turmeric
⅔ teaspoon freshly ground black pepper,
    plus more for the eggs
1 rounded teaspoon garam masala
1½ teaspoons ground coriander
1½ teaspoons ground cumin
salt, to taste
4 teaspoons lemon juice, or to taste
large handful of chopped chives or parsley
    (cilantro is a little strong for this dish)
large handful of roasted cashews (optional)
4 large eggs
pinch of chili powder

Masala baked beans
SERVES 4

My husband's family only eat baked beans like this. Serve on whole wheat toast for brunch.

Heat 2 teaspoons vegetable oil and a good small piece of unsalted butter in a pan. Add 1 small red onion, minced, scant ¼ ounce gingerroot, peeled and grated, and 2 thin green chiles, seeded and minced. Sauté for two minutes. Add 2 large garlic cloves, peeled and grated, and sauté until just coloring. Tip in 2 x 14-ounce cans of baked beans, then fill a can with water and pour this in, too. Bring to a boil and simmer for two minutes. Add generous ⅔ cup grated sharp cheddar, and stir until creamy.

Indians eat spiced potatoes for breakfast in their dosas (a crisp South Indian pancake), and the Parsi people love them sautéed, with eggs on top, but this recipe is inspired by American hashed potatoes. They are lovely with the omelet here but also with Masala Baked Beans (see page 20). This omelet is simply one of my favorite meals, and comes into play well beyond breakfast time. It is cooked until golden on both sides, and is spongy rather than soft. It's truly delicious.

My Indian potato hash and masala omelet

Bring the potatoes to a boil in a pan of water and boil for 15 minutes, or until just cooked through. Once cool enough to handle, grate on the coarse side of a box grater. (I grate the skin too, as I like it and it's full of fiber.) Set aside.

Heat 1 tablespoon of the oil in a nonstick skillet. Add the cumin seeds and, once they start to color and become aromatic, add the onion. Sauté for three to four minutes, or until soft and coloring on the edges, then add the garlic. Cook for another minute or until the garlic is beginning to color. Add everything else except the potato and sauté for 20 seconds. Stir into the potato and mix well. Taste for seasoning and adjust if necessary. Tip out onto a plate, then form the mixture into four evenly sized patties. Wipe out the pan.

Heat the remaining oil in the pan until hot, then add the potato patties and cook, undisturbed, over medium-low heat for two or three minutes, or until golden on the base. Flip over and repeat. Remove them from the pan, placing on paper towels to absorb excess oil.

Meanwhile, mix the onion, tomatoes, chil(es), and cilantro into the eggs and beat again, then season to taste with salt.

Melt a small piece of butter in a nonstick skillet. Pour in one-quarter of the omelet mixture and cook gently, undisturbed, for one to two minutes or until the bottom is golden, then flip over and cook the other side until golden too. I normally slide it onto a plate and then pop it back into the pan to stop it breaking. Serve immediately with a potato hash cake, while you cook the other omelets.

SERVES 4

FOR THE HASH
2 potatoes (around 14 ounces in total), scrubbed well
3 tablespoons vegetable oil
½ teaspoon cumin seeds
1 small red onion, minced
2 small garlic cloves, peeled and minced
½ teaspoon ground cumin
¼ teaspoon chili powder
¼ teaspoon turmeric
½ teaspoon dried mango powder (if you have it)
⅔ teaspoon ground coriander
salt, to taste
2 tablespoons chopped cilantro leaves

FOR THE OMELET
1 red onion, minced
2 small ripe tomatoes, chopped
1–4 green chiles, minced (seeded if you prefer), or to taste
8 tablespoons minced cilantro leaves
8 large eggs, beaten
a few small pieces of unsalted butter

These are eaten with Masala Chai (see below), as biscotti are taken with coffee in Italy. I always ate these cookies at relatives' homes in India; they are quite addictive, not too crunchy, not too soft, and not too sweet. I've rediscovered them recently and they are as addictive now as they were then. I like them plain, but you can further embellish them with nuts as if they were biscotti, if you prefer.

Indian tea cookies

Butter a 7-inch square pan and line with baking parchment. Preheat the oven to 350°F. Beat the sugar and butter until soft and creamy. Beat in the eggs, one at a time. Sift the flour with the baking powder and add to the mixture with the salt and spice, if using. Mix well, then stir in the milk. Pour the batter into the pan, place on the middle shelf of the oven, and cook for 30 to 35 minutes, or until a toothpick in the center comes out clean and it is springy to touch.

Once it is cool enough to handle, halve the cake, then cut across into ¾-inch-thick cookies. Place cut side down on a baking sheet. Reduce the oven temperature to 300°F and bake the cookies for 70 to 80 minutes, or until they are golden with browned edges. (You can bake them for less time for a softer cookie.)

Cool and store in an airtight tin. They last well for two weeks.

MAKES AT LEAST 20

scant ½ cup unsalted butter, softened, plus more for the pan
scant ½ cup superfine sugar
3 eggs
scant 1 cup all-purpose flour
¾ teaspoon baking powder
pinch of salt
½ teaspoon ground cardamom or ginger (optional)
2 tablespoons whole milk

Masala chai

I am a tea drinker and sweet-spiced Indian chai, with a hint of heat from ginger and pepper, is the ultimate revive-relax drink; it is a wondrous thing. I normally make mine with gingerroot and whole spices, but this way is so much quicker and easier that it soon weaves its way into your morning.

Grind together 1½ tablespoons green cardamom pods, 2 teaspoons fennel seeds, 1 rounded teaspoon ground ginger, ½ teaspoon black peppercorns, 6 cloves, and a 1-inch cinnamon stick in a spice or coffee grinder, until you have a fine powder. Store in a jar, away from the sunlight.

To make tea for one, pour 1 cup of water and 3 tablespoons milk into a small pan. Add ½ teaspoon tea leaves and ½ teaspoon of the chai powder. Bring to a boil and simmer until the color of the tea is to your liking. Pour through a small strainer into your cup. Sweeten to taste with sugar and add a little more chai powder if you like.

DRINKS

When I started developing this juice I had no idea how delicious it would be. It reminds me of the fresh sugar cane juice we would get at juice stalls in India, even though I have no idea if the stallholders added ginger to theirs. Indian juices often had a pinch of salt and pepper in them; the salt was to replenish minerals lost through sweat. It doesn't taste salty but seems to heighten the sweet, sour flavor of the fruit. It is of course optional and an acquired taste, though one I associate with my visits to India. You need a sweet, aromatic melon, such as cantaloupe or honeydew.

Melon and ginger sharbat

Blend the melon, ginger, sugar, and orange juice together until smooth. Add the lemon juice if the orange isn't very tart. Adjust the sugar and ginger to taste.

Add salt and pepper for a more authentic experience and pour the sharbat over ice-laden glasses.

SERVES 4

5½ pounds melon flesh
1¼ ounces gingerroot, peeled weight, or to taste
4 teaspoons superfine sugar, or to taste
juice of 2 oranges
squeeze of lemon juice (if necessary)
pinch of salt (optional)
pinch of freshly ground black pepper (optional)
lots of ice

Pomegranate sharbat

Try to buy organic or unwaxed citrus fruits. If these aren't available, scrub the citrus very well to remove wax.
Pour as much pure pomegranate juice into a pitcher, or individual glasses, as you need. Cut thin slices from a lemon, a lime, and an orange. Add to the pitcher with a small fistful of whole mint leaves and let the juice sit for at least 15 minutes to infuse, before serving with ice.

Mangoes are known as the king of fruit in India and, for me, the world. There is nothing better than a mango languorously ripening in my fruit basket, while the sight of boxes of Indian mangoes in springtime cheers me up no end and reminds me of sunnier days to come. There are lots of varieties. Alphonso is my all-time favorite, but there are others that come a close second and third. When making these drinks, use a full-flavored ripe fruit, or you will end up with something merely ordinary. The flavor of mango just needs enhancement, not masking. This is a healthy, easy breakfast for when you are in a hurry or cannot face food first thing in the morning.

Mango, honey, and rose smoothie

Take the flesh off the mangoes: working above your blender, cut the cheeks from the mangoes as close to the seed as possible. Halve these lengthwise. Cut or peel off the skin, making sure the juices flow into the blender. Peel off the skin around the seed and cut off as much as you can of the musky fruit from around it. Add this to the blender, too.

Add everything else and blend until smooth, adding 8–12 tablespoons of water to the blender to help, if necessary. (You may need to do this in batches, to avoid overloading the blender and splattering the kitchen.) Taste, adjust the honey if you want a sweeter drink, and add more water if it is too thick, then serve.

MAKES 4 LARGE GLASSES

4 juicy, ripe mangoes
generous 2¾–scant 3¼ cups yogurt
   (depending how tart it is)
3 teaspoons rose essence or rose water
24 blanched almonds
4 teaspoons honey, or to taste

Saffron "aamraas"
MAKES 4 SMALL GLASSES

"Aam" means mangoes and "raas" means juice. There are many in India who make this as a thick puree and eat it with bread, but I have always had it thinned down as a drink. It's best in small portions with lots of ice, and is a great summer drink to serve in a large pitcher for guests. Saffron may seem an indulgent ingredient here, but it really complements the mango.

   Prepare two mangoes as above. Bring 1¾ cups of milk to a boil with a pinch of saffron, then reduce the heat, simmer, and reduce to half its original quantity, stirring all the time. Then pour onto the mangoes in a blender and blend until smooth. Taste, add 2 teaspoons of superfine sugar if necessary, then chill. To serve, add cold milk or water to reach a consistency you like, and serve on lots of ice.

This traditional lassi is very popular in the northern region of Punjab, where field workers would replenish themselves with both salt and sugar while cooling their bodies with mint and cumin seeds.

Sweet and savory mint lassi

Blend together most of the yogurt with scant 2¼ cups of water, the sugar, salt, cumin, and half the mint. (You may need to do this in two batches, to avoid overloading the blender and splattering the kitchen.)

Stir in the remaining mint, taste, and adjust the sweetness and yogurt. Chill, then serve in glasses with the ice.

SERVES 4

scant 3¼ cups yogurt (if it is quite tart, add 2⅔–generous 2¾ cups and adjust at end)
8 teaspoons superfine sugar, or to taste
pinch of salt
1⅓–2 teaspoons roasted ground cumin (see page 9)
8 tablespoons shredded mint leaves or dried mint, crumbled in, to taste
crushed or shaved ice, to serve

A really lovely, fragrant, and delicate lassi, delicious at any time of the day and with any Indian meal.

Cardamom, almond, and rose lassi

Blend the yogurt, milk, almonds, cardamom, rose water, and sugar together until smooth. (You may need to do this in two batches, to avoid overloading the blender and splattering the kitchen.)

Put the ice and rose petals, if using, into glasses, then pour in the lassi and serve.

SERVES 4

2⅔ cups yogurt (not too sour)
generous 2 cups lowfat milk
24 blanched almonds
1–1½ teaspoons ground cardamom
½–1½ teaspoons rose water, or to taste
4–5 tablespoons superfine sugar, or to taste
handful of crushed ice or ice cubes
organic rose petals (optional)

When visiting India as a teenager, I became obsessed with cold coffee and ice cream. South Indian coffee is delicious and once you added milk, ice cream, and sugar, it was divine ... I suppose it was the original iced frappuccino. I have added cinnamon and cardamom and it is quite wonderful. Like a cherry on top, I like to finish it with a sprinkling of cocoa. I don't have a coffee machine, so I use instant. If you can make fresh coffee at home, use 1¾ cups of strong coffee instead, it will be even better.

Spiced coffee and vanilla float

Stir the coffee into 1¾ cups of boiling water with the sugar and spices. Once well mixed, add the milk. Let cool, then chill.

Once cold, pour into glasses with the ice cubes and scoop the ice cream carefully on top. Sprinkle with a little cocoa or cinnamon. Serve immediately, with a straw and a spoon.

SERVES 4

5 teaspoons instant coffee, or to taste (or filter coffee or espresso, see recipe introduction)
7 teaspoons superfine sugar, or to taste
a few pinches of ground cardamom
1 teaspoon ground cinnamon, or to taste (I like a little more)
2½ cups lowfat milk
8 ice cubes
4 small scoops of good-quality vanilla ice cream
unsweetened cocoa or ground cinnamon, to serve

Iced lemon, ginger, and mint tea
SERVES 3 TO 4

A lovely, refreshing drink for a summer's day in the garden. Once cold, taste and see if you'd like more ginger. Feel free to use your favorite tea bags. Try the drink, without the tea, for children.

Place 2 tea bags (I like Assam) in generous 2 cups of boiling water and let steep for three minutes. Meanwhile, lightly bruise seven or eight ginger slices, skin on, so they release their lovely juices. Squeeze out the water from the tea bags and keep them aside (in case you want the tea stronger at the end). Add scant ½ cup superfine sugar to the tea and stir to dissolve. Add 3 tablespoons of lemon juice and pour the whole thing into a pitcher in which there is a good handful of ice, generous 2 cups of cold water, the ginger, and the leaves from 3–4 sprigs of mint. Stir, then chill. Before serving, add lemon slices, taste, and adjust the sugar (you will need to dissolve any extra sugar in hot water first), lemon, and mint to taste.

APPETIZERS
AND SNACKS

One of India's favorite street foods, this is a deeply satisfying combination of sweet, tangy, spicy, and crunchy. It is typically teatime fare and I often make a large bowl when I have friends over, but I also love to eat a big portion for a light summer lunch. Most Indian stores sell a ready-made bag of bhel mix, consisting of puffed rice, sev (small gram flour vermicelli), and papri (little rounds of crispy dough). If you cannot get this, buy the three items separately. The bhel puri is best assembled just before eating, as the puffed rice softens as it sits, but you can have the elements ready to mix together. You can also buy the chutneys from some Indian grocers if you do not feel like making your own.

Mumbai bhel puri

Have all the ingredients chopped and ready and, when you want to eat, mix the whole thing together, and serve immediately, sprinkled with a little extra sev if you have it.

SERVES 4

Tangy herb chutney
MAKES SCANT 1 CUP

The cornerstone of all North Indian snacks. We love it with samosas, bhajis, pakoras, kebabs … and most other things.

Put 2¼ ounces of cilantro leaves with some of the stalks in a blender, and add 2 tablespoons of lemon juice, 1 seeded green chile, ¾ ounce of mint leaves, scant ¼ cup of pistachios, ½ garlic clove, 1 tablespoon of yogurt, and ½–¾ teaspoons of superfine sugar, to taste. Add 4 tablespoons of water and blend until very smooth and creamy. Taste and adjust the seasoning, adding more chile or sugar as you prefer. Keep in the refrigerator, or freeze, until ready to use.

Instant tamarind chutney
MAKES SCANT ½ CUP

A quick sweet-sour chutney, used in India almost as ketchup is in the west. It keeps well in the refrigerator for a month, or freezes well too.

Put 4 generous teaspoons of good-quality tamarind paste in a small pan with ⅔ cup of water. Add ¼ cup + 2 tablespoons–scant ½ cup of jaggery or dark brown sugar, 1½ teaspoons of roasted cumin seeds (see page 9), and up to ½ teaspoon each of salt and freshly ground black pepper. Bring to a boil and simmer for five to seven minutes, or until it is a little syrupy. It will thicken further as it cools. Taste and adjust the seasoning (different brands of tamarind will vary in strength and tartness), then serve, or store in the refrigerator, or freeze.

8 ounces bhel puri mix (if you can't get the mix, see recipe introduction)
large handful of roasted peanuts, skins removed by rolling between your palms
1 large-ish potato, cooked and finely chopped
1 small red onion, minced
1 tomato, finely chopped
large handful of chopped cilantro leaves
1–2 green chiles, seeded and chopped
¾ tablespoon lemon juice, or to taste
1½ tablespoons Tangy Herb Chutney (see left)
3 tablespoon Instant Tamarind Chutney (see below left)
pomegranate seeds (optional but lovely)
handful of sev, to serve (optional)

These are absolutely delicious and easy to make with simple everyday ingredients (gram flour is a must in all vegetarian households). They are soft and creamy on the inside but with a lovely crisp exterior. I use a good-quality, thick Greek yogurt and cheddar cheese instead of the traditional paneer, to add a lovely savory element. Eat these as they are, or with Basil Chutney (see below).

Savory yogurt kebabs

The night before, put the Greek yogurt in a strainer lined with cheesecloth, place over a bowl, and leave in the refrigerator overnight.

The next day, add the gram flour to a nonstick skillet and stir over gentle heat until it has a toasted smell and turns a golden color, four to five minutes. Scrape into a large bowl. Clean the pan and heat 1 tablespoon of the oil. Add the onion; cook gently until just softened. Add the garlic, ginger, and salt and cook until the garlic no longer smells raw, 40 to 50 seconds. Stir in the garam masala and roasted ground cumin, take off the heat, and add to the gram flour with the drained yogurt, cheese, three-quarters of the bread crumbs, the cilantro, green chile, and black pepper. Stir well and season to taste. It should be creamy but firm enough to roll into balls. If not, add more crumbs. Give the skillet a good wipe.

Heat half the remaining oil in the skillet until hot. Make little balls of the mixture, flatten, and add a batch to the skillet. Cook over gentle heat until the bases are golden brown. Flip over and cook until this side is golden too. Drain on paper towels. Repeat, using more oil and kebabs, until they are all cooked. Serve with Basil Chutney (see below).

MAKES 10 TO 12 SMALL KEBABS

scant 1 cup Greek yogurt
generous ½ cup gram (chickpea) flour
3 tablespoons vegetable oil
½ onion, minced
2 garlic cloves, peeled and minced
scant ½ ounce gingerroot, peeled weight, minced
salt, to taste
¾ teaspoon garam masala, or to taste
½ teaspoon roasted ground cumin (see page 9)
¼ cup finely grated sharp cheddar cheese
2 slices of white bread, crumbed, plus more if needed
2 tablespoons chopped cilantro leaves
½–1 green chile, seeded and minced (optional)
freshly ground black pepper

Basil chutney
MAKES ENOUGH TO GO WITH THE KEBABS

You'll need a really large bunch of basil for this; it should weigh about 3 ounces.
Pick the leaves from the basil and place in a mini food processor. Add 15 pistachios, 1 small garlic clove, peeled, and 1½ tablespoons of extra virgin olive oil. Process, adding a splash of water to help the blades go around if necessary. Taste, and adjust the seasoning with lemon juice.

I first ate a momo when a Nepalese lady was helping me at home with my first baby six years ago. She did lots of chopping, then 10 minutes later had made her momos. I am dumpling-obsessed, so have dreamed of homemade momos ever since. They were brought to India by Tibetan and Nepalese people and, every time I go to Kolkata, I am tempted by the momo street vendors and restaurants catering solely to dumpling lovers. Making them is not as hard as it might seem, although your first momo will probably look quite different to your last! (See the previous page for step-by-step photos of the process.) The chutney served with this is really spicy; below is my version, but feel free to experiment.

Steamed Nepalese momos

Mix the flour with 2 tablespoons of water and make a dough. Give it a good knead so it is smooth and soft, adding 1 teaspoon more water if needed. Halve the dough and roll each half into a long rope. Pinch off equal tiny portions, aiming to get seven or eight from each rope. Roll each into a smooth ball and cover with a damp dish towel.

Mix all the ingredients for the filling, taste, and adjust the seasoning.

Place a steamer filled with water on the heat and oil the steamer basket. Taking one ball of dough at a time, use a little flour to roll out into a very thin 2½–3-inch circle. Place a generous teaspoonful of filling in the center. Take the momo in your left hand (if right handed) and use your thumb and index finger to enclose the filling by gathering the edges of the dough and pleating them together (or you can pleat them to look like rosebuds, see previous page). Either way, make sure the filling stays well away from the edges. Place on the oiled rack, seam side up.

Once they are all done, place in the steamer, close the lid, and steam for 12 to 14 minutes, or until the dough is no longer sticky, then serve.

MAKES 15 TO16 DUMPLINGS

FOR THE DUMPLINGS
⅓ cup all-purpose flour, plus more to dust
a little vegetable oil

FOR THE FILLING
½ onion, minced
3¼ ounces cabbage, finely grated, excess water squeezed out
½ small carrot, finely grated, excess water squeezed out
small handful of frozen peas, defrosted
3 tablespoons finely chopped red pepper
3 fine green beans, finely sliced
¼ ounce gingerroot, peeled weight, minced
2 garlic cloves, peeled and grated
1½ teaspoons soft unsalted butter
½ teaspoon salt, or to taste
good grinding of black pepper

Chili, ginger, and tomato chutney
MAKES ENOUGH TO GO WITH THE MOMOS

Heat 1 tablespoon of vegetable oil in a small pan. Add 3 peeled garlic cloves, generous ½ ounce of gingerroot, peeled weight, and 2–3 green chiles, all roughly chopped, and sauté until the garlic begins to color. Add 2 large tomatoes, roughly chopped, and salt, cover, and cook down until the moisture has evaporated and the tomatoes are darkening. Add some boiled water and blend together (it doesn't have to be too fine). Add 1 teaspoon of minced ginger and 1 tablespoon of chopped cilantro leaves. Taste, adjust the seasoning, and add more finely diced green chile, if you like. It should be loose but not watery, quite hot, and gingery and slightly salty, as the dumplings are simple.

A much-loved snack or appetizer. I find myself returning to them even though there are newer recipes to choose from. They are crisp and delicious and best served hot in batches as soon as they are done. I have paired them with this lovely caper berry chutney. I absolutely love capers and they are particularly fabulous here. If you don't have any capers, you can add a little more lemon juice to the chutney instead.

Crisp onion bhajis with caper berry chutney

Heat 2 inches of vegetable oil in a small pan.

Meanwhile, mix everything else together with your hands, squeezing the onions enough to allow their juices to come out and soften the gram flour. Form the mixture into small walnut-sized balls.

Check that the oil is ready by dropping in a little of the batter; it should start sizzling straightaway. Add the balls to the hot oil in two batches. Reduce the heat to medium-low and cook for seven to eight minutes, turning, or until deep golden brown all over. Remove with a slotted spoon and drain on paper towels. Serve piping hot with the chutney, while you cook the next batch.

MAKES 12

vegetable oil, to deep-fry
2 red onions, finely sliced
4 tablespoons chopped cilantro leaves
salt, to taste
½–¾ teaspoon chili powder
½ teaspoon turmeric
1 teaspoon garam masala
2 teaspoons ground coriander
2 teaspoons dried mango powder
2 teaspoons ground cumin
generous 1 cup gram (chickpea) flour
2 garlic cloves, peeled and grated
½ ounce gingerroot, peeled weight, grated
⅓ teaspoon cumin seeds

Caper berry chutney
MAKES ⅔ CUP

Blend 1¼ ounces of cilantro leaves and stalks with ¾ ounce of mint leaves, 1–2 green chiles, seeded, scant ¼ cup of pistachios, 2 teaspoons of lemon juice, 2 tablespoons of water, and 2 tablespoons of small caper berries.

Adjust the seasoning. Stir in 1 tablespoon of capers. Adjust the lemon, water, and salt to taste (though you probably won't need salt) and serve, or refrigerate for up to a few days.

In these wonderful little cakes, the beet is absolutely delicious and surprises everyone who tries them. I often serve them with this Kashmiri-inspired radish and yogurt "chutney." I very rarely use a microwave but, when it comes to cooking potatoes in a hurry without them absorbing too much moisture, it's the ideal method.

Mini beet cakes with radish and yogurt 'chutney'

Heat half the oil in a nonstick skillet. Add the onion and sauté for two minutes. Add the ginger and garlic and sauté until the garlic smells cooked and turns lightly golden.

Grate the beet, squeeze out the excess juice (I squeeze it over a cup and drink the fresh beet juice as I cook), and add to the pan with the garam masala, cumin, chili powder, and salt. Sauté until the moisture dries up, then add a good splash of water, cover, and cook until the beet is just soft, adding more splashes of water as you need; it can take around 30 minutes. Cook off all the excess moisture. Add the cooked potato and mash the whole thing together; it doesn't have to be smooth. Cook off any excess moisture if the mixture seems wet.

Put the mixture on a plate and wipe the pan clean. Make little cakes out of the mix, about 1¼ inches wide and ½ inch thick. Heat the remaining oil in the pan and add the cakes. Cook over medium heat until they are lightly crisp on the base but have not colored too much. Turn over and cook for another two to three minutes. Meanwhile, stir together all the ingredients for the chutney and season to taste. Serve the beet cakes with a little of the chutney on top.

MAKES 12 TO 14

FOR THE BEET CAKES
3 tablespoons vegetable oil
1 small red onion, chopped
2 rounded teaspoons peeled, grated
   gingerroot
2 garlic cloves, peeled and grated
9 ounces small-ish raw beet, peeled
½–¾ teaspoon garam masala, or to taste
good pinch of cumin or caraway seeds
¼ teaspoon chili powder, or to taste,
   plus a little more to serve
salt, to taste
2 potatoes, cooked and peeled
   (see recipe introduction)

FOR THE RADISH AND YOGURT "CHUTNEY"
3 large radishes, coarsely grated
scant ½ cup Greek yogurt
¼ cup crème fraîche
2 tablespoons minced cilantro leaves
1 scallion, green part only, finely sliced
1 green chile, seeded and chopped (optional)

Mini chili cheese toasts
MAKES 12 TO 14 SMALL TOASTS

I've never met anyone who doesn't like these. You can serve big slices of it for lunch, with a green salad.

Preheat the oven to its highest setting. Slice a baguette ½ inch thick. Place on the upper oven shelf to toast. Mix ¾ small red onion, minced, 1 small tomato, finely chopped, ¼–½ green chile, minced, 2 tablespoons of chopped cilantro leaves, a pinch of salt, and generous 1 cup of grated cheddar. Mound onto the toasts and cook until the cheese melts and there are a few speckled brown bits on top. Bits of the cheese will spill onto the baking sheet. They're my favorite!

Fluffy, spongy, savory cakes from the region of Gujarat. These are made with yellow lentils (mung dal), which are really light and mild in flavor, so perfect once steeped in this spicy rasam broth. You need an 8-inch round cake pan with a fixed bottom and a large, deep pan or wok with a lid, into which such a cake pan will fit. Then you need to find something on which to place the pan so that it does not touch the water. Any heatproof bowl (I use ovenproof bowls) or colander will work.

Steamed lentil cakes in sweet, spicy, sour rasam

Drain the soaked lentils and put them in a blender (or put them in a bowl and use a stick blender). Add the ginger, chiles, salt, sugar, oil, lemon juice, and scant ½ cup of water and blend to a paste. Mix in the baking soda and leave for 15 minutes.

Meanwhile, find a wide, large double boiler or deep and large pan, big enough to take your cake pan. Find something to place the pan on, so its bottom is above the level of the water (ovenproof bowls, steel baking rings, and upturned colanders are all good). Pour in enough water to come 2 inches up the pan. Cover the pan tightly and bring to a boil.

Pour the batter into an oiled 8-inch cake pan, place it carefully on its stand in the pan, cover, and steam until an inserted toothpick comes out clean, 10 to 12 minutes. Take off the lid, let the steam escape, and carefully take out the pan (I use oven mitts and tongs).

For the rasam, heat the oil in a small nonstick pan. Add the mustard seeds and, once the popping is dying down, add the curry leaves. Follow a few seconds later with the tomato, spices, and salt. Cook over high–moderate heat for three to four minutes, stirring often, then add scant ⅔ cup of water. Bring to a boil, reduce the heat, and simmer for 10 minutes. Stir in the sugar and tamarind and simmer for another minute; it should be a little sweet, sour, and spicy. Adjust the salt, sugar, chili powder, and tamarind as you like. Turn off the heat.

Cut the lentil cake into 2-inch squares or half moons, place in deep warmed bowls, and spoon over a little of the rasam. Let soak for four to five minutes, then sprinkle with cilantro and coconut, if you have some, and serve.

SERVES 4

FOR THE LENTIL CAKES

1 cup yellow lentils (mung dal), washed well and soaked overnight

¼ ounce gingerroot, peeled weight

2 thin green chiles, stalks removed and seeded

1 rounded teaspoon salt, or to taste

3 teaspoons superfine sugar

1 tablespoon vegetable oil, plus more for the pan

1 tablespoon lemon juice

⅔ teaspoon baking soda

FOR THE RASAM

1 tablespoon vegetable oil

¾ teaspoon mustard seeds

8 fresh curry leaves (or 12 dried)

1 large tomato, chopped

2 teaspoons ground coriander

1 teaspoon ground cumin

½–¾ teaspoon chili powder, or to taste

salt, to taste

1–1½ tablespoons superfine sugar, to taste

1½–1¾ teaspoons tamarind paste dissolved in 3 tablespoons boiling water, or to taste

cilantro leaves, to serve (optional)

fresh, or frozen and defrosted, grated coconut, to serve (optional)

A restaurant vegetarian favorite, these are normally tunneled out and stuffed with a mixture of paneer, cashews, raisins, and the fried potato scraps. This was the initial inspiration for this dish, but these are much easier, lighter, and tastier. They make great, easy appetizers or a wonderful side dish, if made with larger potatoes, for a barbecue.

Tandoori baby potatoes with herb yogurt

Peel the potatoes and halve. Bring lots of salted water to a boil in a large pan. Add the potatoes and boil for eight minutes. Remove and, when cool enough to handle, use a spoon to scrape out a deep depression so that the potatoes look like boiled egg halves where the yolk has been removed.

Mix the ingredients for the tandoori marinade in a bowl. Add one good teaspoon of salt (the marinade only coats the potato so the salt will not seem excessive). Place the potato halves in the bowl, turn to coat in the marinade, and let marinate for 30 minutes. Mix together all the ingredients for the topping, adding the milk if the consistency seems a little thick, and season to taste.

Preheat the oven to 425°F. Place the potatoes, flat side up, on a baking sheet and place on the middle shelf of the oven. Cook for 20 to 25 minutes, or until the marinade looks properly dried. Now turn the potatoes over, move the rack to the top of the oven, and continue to cook for eight to 10 minutes. Turn again and cook for a final eight to 10 minutes. They should be tender by now (check by piercing one of the largest potato halves with a knife).

Meanwhile, melt the butter and brush it over the potatoes. Spoon a rounded teaspoon of topping onto each potato half and serve immediately.

MAKES 16 HALVES

FOR THE POTATOES
8 baby potatoes
salt
2 tablespoons unsalted butter

FOR THE TANDOORI MARINADE
⅔ cup Greek yogurt
1¾ teaspoons ground cumin
¾ teaspoon garam masala
1 teaspoon ground coriander
¼–½ teaspoon chili powder
1 teaspoon paprika
3 garlic cloves, peeled and grated
scant ¼ ounce gingerroot, peeled weight, grated
2 tablespoons vegetable oil
1½ tablespoons lemon juice, or to taste

FOR THE TOPPING
generous 1 cup Greek yogurt
⅓ teaspoon freshly ground black pepper
good handful of chopped cilantro leaves
½–¾ small onion, minced
1 green chile, seeded and minced, or to taste
2 tablespoons dried cranberries or raisins (optional, for a sweet/savory combination)
1–2 tablespoons whole milk, if needed

I loved Scotch eggs when I visited England in my summer vacations as a teenager. I wanted them for a snack, on picnics, and as part of my lunch! They were so very British to me. So British, in fact, that they were brought to Kolkata during the Raj and can now be seen on some menus in that corner of India. I use quail's eggs, but you can use hen's eggs instead and serve them with a salad for lunch or brunch. If you do not eat eggs, make this vegetarian sausagemeat into kebabs instead: add a diced tomato to the mixture, shape onto skewers, and cook in the oven or in a skillet.

Scotch quail's eggs

Heat 2 teaspoons of the oil in a small nonstick skillet and fry the garlic until coloring. Then tip into a blender with the ginger and drained lentils and blend until smooth. Do not add any water.

Heat the remaining oil in the skillet. Add the lentil paste and cook over medium-low heat for six to seven minutes, turning often. The mixture gets tough, but you need to persevere. I spread it out in the skillet, let it cook for 10 seconds, turn it, then repeat. Keep moving and squashing it with a spoon so it cooks evenly. There is no elegant technique!

Take off the heat, add the remaining ingredients except the eggs, and mix well together; it will resemble a dough. Let cool. At this point, you can cover the mixture and chill overnight, if it's more convenient. When you're ready to make the Scotch eggs, boil the quail's eggs for four minutes, then plunge into cold water to stop the cooking.

Peel the eggs. Take around 1–1¼ ounces of the lentil mixture and flatten it in your palm. Place an egg in the middle and envelop it with the mixture. (It is easier than it sounds.) Repeat with the rest.

Meanwhile, heat 1¼ inches of vegetable oil in a small pan and heat to about 350°F or until, when a scrap of bread is dropped in, it sizzles immediately but does not brown. Add the eggs, in batches, and cook over moderate heat until they are golden all over.

Remove with a slotted spoon and drain on paper towels. Keep warm while you fry the remaining eggs, and serve hot as they are, or with a little Southern Tomato Chutney (see page 128).

MAKES 12

4 tablespoons vegetable oil, plus more to deep-fry
4 garlic cloves, peeled and roughly sliced
¾ ounce gingerroot, peeled weight
1 cup red lentils (masoor dal), washed well and soaked overnight
2 large slices of bread, crumbed
1½ teaspoons garam masala
1 teaspoon salt
large pinch of freshly ground black pepper
1½ teaspoons ground cumin
1 teaspoon chili powder
2 teaspoons lemon juice
2 tablespoons Greek yogurt
2 large shallots, minced (or ½ onion)
4 tablespoons minced cilantro leaves
12 quail's eggs

I have always loved artichokes, but had never cooked an Indian dish with them until I invented this recipe recently. The gram flour batter adds a layer of flavor which is sympathetic to the artichokes. It is daunting to prepare an artichoke if you haven't done it before, but you get used to it quickly (see below). I am quite happy to munch on these with a squeeze of lemon juice alone, but they also work with Tangy Herb Chutney (see page 34), or even a lovely garlicky mayonnaise.

Indian-style artichoke fritti

Whisk together the ingredients for the batter with scant ¾–scant 1 cup of water until smooth. Taste and adjust the salt and chili powder.

Heat 2 inches of oil in a wide, medium pan. Dip the artichoke slices into the batter and, using tongs, place gently in the hot oil, one at a time. Do not overcrowd the pan. Cook on moderate heat, turning once, until the batter is deep golden on both sides, it should take three to four minutes. Drain and place on a double layer of paper towels. Repeat with the remaining artichoke slices. Serve immediately, with lemon wedges.

SERVES 4

FOR THE BATTER
⅔ cup gram (chickpea) flour
salt, to taste
1 teaspoon peeled, grated gingerroot
1 teaspoon grated garlic
½ teaspoon chili powder, or to taste
1 teaspoon garam masala
2 slightly rounded teaspoons ground coriander
2 slightly rounded teaspoons ground cumin
½ teaspoon turmeric
2 teaspoons dried mango powder

FOR THE REST
vegetable oil, to deep-fry
2 large globe artichokes, prepared as below and sliced ¼ inch thick
lemon wedges, to serve

How to prepare an artichoke

Fill a bowl with water and add the juice of ½ lemon. Working on one artichoke at a time, remove all the dark green leaves. (I slice through the tops then pluck out the tough green leaves until I'm left with thin, paler leaves.) Pluck these off as well, or slice through their bases with a knife. Now remove the furry choke from the center; I find this comes out with a good scraping with a spoon, taking out all the (deceptively) soft fibers. The cut surface will start to oxidize and brown immediately, so rub it with the other lemon half to prevent discoloration. Slice off and discard most of the stem, leaving ¾–1¾ inches; peel off its tough green skin. Place straight in the lemony water until ready to use.

SALADS, BROILS, AND GRILLS

This is a really fresh, vibrant, and fruity salad with the grown-up edge of ginger and chile. A good, ripe mango is important as it will add vibrancy and set off the crumbly, creamy paneer. I make my own paneer as it's easy and much creamier than store bought (see page 9 for how to make it), but I leave it up to you. You can substitute mozzarella (don't broil it, of course). Lastly, find good-quality sun-dried tomatoes. I buy mine from a deli; they are more sun-blushed than dried and are moist and fresh.

Broiled paneer and mango salad with ginger dressing

Put the broiler on. Whisk together the ingredients for the dressing. Make sure the sugar and salt have dissolved and the whole thing emulsifies.

If your paneer is not fresh, soak in boiling water until it softens, around 10 minutes. Then toss it in a little olive oil and season with salt and pepper. Place on an oiled rack and broil until it has browned on the edges, around seven to 10 minutes. (You can also griddle the paneer in a hot griddle pan.)

Meanwhile, toss the remaining salad ingredients with the dressing, either all together or separately, depending on how you want to present the salad. When the paneer is done, place on top. Serve immediately.

SERVES 4

FOR THE GINGER DRESSING
6–8 teaspoons lemon juice, to taste
6 tablespoons olive oil, plus more for the paneer
salt, to taste
2 teaspoons superfine sugar, or to taste
¾ ounce gingerroot, peeled weight, finely grated

FOR THE SALAD
11 ounces paneer (preferably homemade, see page 9), cut into long flat rectangles or other shapes
freshly ground black pepper
4 large handfuls of baby spinach or mixed salad greenss
1 cup sun-dried tomatoes in oil
2 large or 4 small ripe mangoes, cheeks cut off and diced into ⅝-inch pieces
½ small red onion, finely sliced
1 mild red chile, finely sliced (optional)
handful of chopped cilantro leaves
handful of roasted peanuts or cashews

This lovely, light dish started out as a simple zucchini carpaccio on a summer evening when I had friends coming over. It has since morphed into a more substantial dish that works equally well as a light salad or as a platter to be eaten with broiled foods. Griddling zucchini slices adds a lot of flavor. The Indian-inspired chickpea salsa is based upon a roadside chaat, but is fresher.

Griddled zucchini carpaccio, chickpea salsa, pistachio dressing

Heat a griddle or stovetop grill pan until quite hot. Slice the zucchini on the diagonal into thin slices, no more than ¼ inch thick. Oil the slices, place on the griddle in a single layer, and cook, undisturbed, for three minutes, or until the base has well-charred lines. Turn and repeat on the other side. Repeat with the remaining zucchini. Transfer to a plate as you cook each batch.

As you stand over the griddle, stir together the chickpeas, lemon juice, roasted cumin, tomato, and red onion and season to taste.

Blend together all the ingredients for the dressing with 2 tablespoons water until smooth; I use a good stick blender, but a mortar and pestle will also work. Adjust the seasoning and vinegar to taste and set aside.

To assemble, place the zucchini on plates or a platter, slightly overlapping at the edges. Drizzle with the dressing. Mix the cilantro into the chickpeas, scatter them over with the feta cheese, and serve.

SERVES 4 AS A SIDE DISH, OR 2 AS A LIGHT LUNCH

FOR THE SALAD

4 large zucchini (a mix of green and yellow, if possible)

olive oil, to brush

14-ounce can chickpeas, drained well and rinsed

1½ tablespoons lemon juice, or to taste

1 scant tablespoon roasted ground cumin (see page 9)

1 small tomato, finely chopped

⅓–½ small red onion, minced

salt, to taste

1¼ ounces cilantro (leaves and roots), chopped

3–3½ ounces feta cheese, crumbled

FOR THE PISTACHIO DRESSING

¾–1 tablespoon red or white wine vinegar, or to taste

1 small garlic clove, peeled

2 tablespoons pistachios (roasted is fine)

2½ tablespoons extra virgin olive oil

¼ teaspoon coarsely ground black pepper, or to taste

¼ teaspoon superfine sugar

This lovely dish is a fusion of a creamy American potato salad and the potato salad from India known as aloo chaat. Chaat masala is a blend of tangy spices and literally means "to lick" (as in your fingers). It can be found in all Indian grocers, as well as online. You can leave it out if you don't have it, the salad is still sublime without overpowering the potatoes. Any waxy potatoes will work in this salad, so find out what is in season and use those as they will have the best flavor. The radishes add bite and crunch and their leaves have a lovely peppery flavor, but you can add any other vegetable you like; try finely sliced fennel, cucumbers, celery, or even fine green beans.

Three-seed potato salad

Place the potatoes in a large pot and cover with plenty of water, salt well, and bring to a boil. Boil until the tip of a knife goes through them easily, around 15 minutes.

Meanwhile, make the dressing. Whisk together the lemon juice, mayonnaise, sour cream, garlic, and half the oil, then season to taste. Heat the remaining oil in a small pan, tilting it so the oil collects in one area. When hot, add the mustard and cumin seeds, following after a few seconds with the fennel seeds. Reduce the heat and cook for 10 seconds or until the popping dies down. Stir into the dressing.

Drain the cooked potatoes and peel as soon as they are cool enough to handle; halve if small, or quarter larger ones. Stir into the dressing with the red onion, chiles, and chaat masala, if using. The potatoes will absorb the dressing as they cool. Stir in the radishes and their leaves and the cilantro just before serving. Taste and adjust the seasoning. Sprinkle with a little more chaat masala, if you like, then serve.

SERVES 4 AS A SIDE DISH

FOR THE SALAD
1 pound 2 ounces new potatoes, washed well
salt, to taste
¼ small red onion, very finely sliced
1–2 green chiles, seeded and minced (optional)
½–¾ teaspoon chaat masala, plus more to serve (optional, see recipe introduction)
3 large radishes with leaves (if possible), well washed and finely sliced
large handful of chopped cilantro leaves

FOR THE DRESSING
2 teaspoons lemon juice
4 tablespoons mayonnaise (light is fine)
2 rounded tablespoons sour cream
1 small-ish garlic clove, peeled and grated
1½ tablespoons extra virgin olive oil
lots of freshly ground black pepper
½ teaspoon mustard seeds
½ teaspoon cumin seeds
½ teaspoon fennel seeds

Heirloom tomato and cannellini salad
SERVES 4

Heirloom tomatoes are a motley crew. Happily, they taste great too. Serve this with griddled rustic bread.

Blend 6 tablespoons of extra virgin olive oil, 3 tablespoons of red wine vinegar, 1 garlic clove, and 1–2 seeded red chiles until smooth, then add salt and ¾ teaspoon of superfine sugar. Cut 1¼ pounds heirloom or baby tomatoes into wedges. Stir in ½ sliced red onion with 5 tablespoons of dressing. Mix in 1½ cups of cooked cannellini beans. Toss 4 handfuls of mixed salad greens in a little seasoning and oil. Divide the tomato and beans between four plates. Mound the greens on top. Break ⅔ cup of goat curd or soft goat cheese in chunks and place on top. Grind on pepper, drizzle with more dressing, and serve.

This dried fig chutney is the perfect partner to salty, slightly squeaky Middle Eastern halloumi, though it would be wonderful with most other cheeses as well. I serve this as a light meal with herbed naan on the side, or as part of my Tandoori Vegetable Feast (see page 73). The cheese is also great with Warm Puy Lentils (see page 152) on a bed of lettuce. Panch phoran is a mixture of seeds; if you don't have it, use equal quantities of cumin, nigella, mustard, and fennel seeds.

Spice-crusted halloumi with fig and pistachio chutney

For the chutney, heat the oil in a small nonstick pan. Add the fennel seeds and chili powder, cook for 20 seconds, then add the onion and sauté for two or three minutes. Add the ginger and garlic and cook for another minute or until the garlic is coloring a little. Add the figs, vinegar, sugar, and remaining spices along with a splash of water. Bring to a boil, then cover and cook until the figs are soft and the whole thing has come together. Taste and adjust the seasoning, seeing if you would like more sugar, vinegar, or chili powder. Blend half the chutney together until smooth, then return it to the pan and mix it with the chunky chutney. Stir in the pistachios and set aside.

Cut the halloumi into long ½-inch-thick slices. Sprinkle a little of the panch phoran on one side. Heat a pan and add the oil. Add the halloumi spice side down and cook until golden on the edges, around one or two minutes. Flip over and cook this side in the same way.

Whisk together the extra virgin oil and lemon juice and season with salt and pepper. Toss the salad greens gently in this dressing and serve with the cheese and some fig chutney on the side.

SERVES 4

FOR THE CHUTNEY
1 tablespoon vegetable oil
½ teaspoon fennel seeds
¼ teaspoon chili powder, or to taste
½ small onion, chopped
¼ ounce gingerroot, peeled weight, minced
2 garlic cloves, peeled and grated
3½ ounces dried figs, finely chopped
3½ tablespoons red wine vinegar, or to taste
2 teaspoons superfine sugar, or to taste
⅓ teaspooon garam masala
⅓ teaspoon roasted ground cumin (see page 9)
small fistful of pistachios

FOR THE HALLOUMI
9-ounce package of halloumi
1 tablespoon panch phoran (see recipe introduction)
2 teaspoons vegetable oil
2 tablespoons extra virgin olive oil
¾ tablespoon lemon juice
salt, to taste
freshly ground black pepper
4 handfuls of salad greens

Kathi rolls are one of India's indigenous "sandwiches," in which a filling is encased in bread and designed to be eaten on the go. I was first introduced to the concept in Mumbai, when local friends would stop to buy one from a street vendor who came to the car window. They were always hot, fresh, and absolutely delicious. I haven't had one for years and don't know if the "Frankie seller" still operates, but the memory lives on. I have used a tortilla wrap here, instead of flatbread. You can use any vegetable that is not too watery and retains its texture and flavor.

Mushroom and vegetable kathi rolls

Heat 2½ tablespoons of the oil in a large nonstick skillet. Add the ginger and garlic and cook for one minute, or until the garlic is turning golden.

Add the mushrooms, vegetables, and spices and a little salt. Stir-fry for five to seven minutes, or until the vegetables are cooked but still crispy. Place in a bowl and cover to keep warm. Wipe the pan clean.

Heat 1 teaspoon more vegetable oil in the pan, brush or spoon a good coating of egg on one side of a tortilla, and place in the oil, egg side down; cook for 30 seconds or until the egg is cooked. Turn the tortilla over and cook for 30 seconds or so. Repeat with the other tortillas.

Spoon one-quarter of the filling onto each tortilla, egg side up, and cover evenly with a good tablespoon of chutney. Wrap well, halve, and serve, or wrap in wax paper, tearing down as you eat on the go.

MAKES 4

4 tablespoons vegetable oil
½ ounce gingerroot, peeled weight, grated
4 garlic cloves, peeled and grated
16 cremini mushrooms, cleaned and thickly sliced
1 small-ish red onion, sliced
3 ounces carrot, cut into 2-inch-long thin sticks
12 fine green beans, cut into 2-inch-long pieces
5½ ounces white cabbage, shredded
½ red bell pepper, seeded and sliced lengthwise into fine thin sticks
1½ teaspoons chaat masala (see page 58), or to taste
1 teaspoon ground cumin
1 teaspoon ground coriander
⅔ teaspoon turmeric
salt, to taste
4 flour tortillas
2 small eggs, beaten with a pinch of salt
4 rounded tablespoons Tangy Herb Chutney (see page 34)

Roasting or broiling mushrooms really intensifies their flavors as the heat drives out the moisture. These, in particular, are really delicious; meaty, spicy, and even better if you can barbecue them, as it will add smokiness. They make a lovely appetizer or light meal, but they can be served without the bread crumbs, arugula, or sauce as part of a Tandoori Vegetable Feast (see page 73).

Roasted spiced portobello with creamy lemon dressing

For the crumbs, heat the butter and oil in a large skillet. Add the garlic and fry gently until it starts to color. Add the crumbs and stir-fry over moderate heat until they turn golden. Take off the heat and stir in the herbs. Season to taste.

Whisk together all the ingredients for the dressing and season to taste. Blend together the ingredients for the marinade until smooth and season well. Clean the mushrooms: I like to wash them properly, as there is nothing worse than biting into gritty mushrooms. Poke through the mushrooms in several places with a small sharp blade or skewer and place them in a shallow bowl with the marinade, turning to coat on all sides. Set aside and marinate for at least 30 minutes, though an hour is better if you have the time.

Preheat the oven to 400°F. Put the marinated mushrooms, gill side up, on a baking sheet and roast on the upper shelf, turning halfway, for 12 to 15 minutes. They should look a little shriveled at the edges.

Take out, sprinkle the gill side liberally with the crumbs, place a small fistful of arugula, on the side, and drizzle both with the dressing.

MAKES 4

FOR THE GARLIC HERB CRUMBS
1 tablespoon unsalted butter
1 teaspoon olive oil
1 fat garlic clove, peeled and grated
3 slices of bread, crumbed (not too fine)
1 rounded tablespoon chopped cilantro leaves
1 tablespoon chopped mint leaves
salt, to taste
freshly ground black pepper

FOR THE DRESSING
1½ teaspoons lemon juice
1 scant tablespoon sour cream
3 large mint leaves, shredded
2 tablespoons extra virgin olive oil

FOR THE MARINADE
2 large-ish garlic cloves, peeled
¼ ounce gingerroot, peeled weight
⅓ teaspoon chili powder
¾ teaspoon garam masala
¾ teaspoon ground cumin
2 tablespoons lemon juice
4–5 tablespoons olive oil

FOR THE MUSHROOMS
4 large-ish portobello mushrooms
  (brown-skinned are better)
2 large handfuls of baby arugula leaves

Creamy dipping sauce
MAKES AROUND SCANT 1 CUP

Great with tandoori food, naan, and even baked potatoes.
  Put ⅔ cup of light cream cheese in a bowl and mix together with 2–3 tablespoons of milk. Season well, adding a good handful of chopped cilantro leaves, ½ small onion, minced, 1 green chile, seeded and minced, and 1 teaspoon of lemon juice. Taste, adjust the seasoning, and serve.

These burgers are spicy and deeply satisfying. Put aside any preconceptions of bland, mass-produced bean burgers, these are so much more. The coleslaw really adds vivacity with its texture, freshness, and tanginess. The patties also work well made into kebabs and rolled into a wrap with the coleslaw, Tangy Herb Chutney (see page 34), and garlic yogurt.

Mile-high chickpea burgers with Indian purple coleslaw

For the burgers, heat 2 tablespoons of the oil in a nonstick pan. Add the cumin seeds and cook for 10 to 20 seconds, or until they have darkened a little. Add the onion and cook until golden and the edges are beginning to brown. Add the ginger and garlic and cook gently for a minute or until the garlic no longer smells raw. Add the spices, salt, and a splash of water and cook down until dry again.

Add the chickpeas and cook for three to four minutes, or until most of the moisture in the pan has dried off. Taste and adjust the seasoning. Pour just over three-quarters of the contents of the pan into a blender with the bread crumbs, and blend until smooth. Lightly crush the remaining chickpeas in the pan, scrape the blended mixture back into the pan, and mix well.

Mix together all the ingredients for the coleslaw and season to taste.

When you are ready to eat, heat the remaining oil in a nonstick skillet. Make four to six burgers out of the chickpea mixture, making sure the edges are smooth. Place in the skillet and cook over gentle heat for six to eight minutes, turning once, until both sides are lightly browned.

Meanwhile, lightly toast your buns. Assemble the burgers as you prefer, with the coleslaw, lettuce, and tomato. Balance the remaining bun half on it all and enjoy.

MAKES 4 LARGE BURGERS, OR 6 MEDIUM BURGERS

FOR THE BURGERS

4 tablespoons vegetable oil
1½ teaspoons cumin seeds
1 small-ish onion, minced
2 rounded teaspoons peeled, minced gingerroot
4 garlic cloves, peeled and minced
2 teaspoons ground coriander
1½ teaspoons ground cumin
1½ teaspoons garam masala
1½ teaspoons dried pomegranate powder (optional but really delicious)
1½ teaspoons chili powder
salt, to taste
2 x 14-ounce cans chickpeas, drained and rinsed
2 slices of whole wheat bread, crumbed

FOR THE PURPLE COLESLAW

½ cup shredded red cabbage
scant ¼ cup finely sliced red onion
¼ cup finely sliced carrots
large handful of chopped cilantro leaves
generous ⅓ cup mayonnaise (light is fine)
2 tablespoons Greek yogurt
2 teaspoons lemon juice
freshly ground black pepper

TO SERVE

4 large, or 6 small, burger buns (I like those with sesame seeds on top)
a few crispy lettuce leaves
1 large vine tomato, sliced

This is a really popular Delhi street food and, once corn season arrives, you will find mounds of cobs on makeshift carts along the roadside, all being grilled over charcoal until the kernels are charred and lightly blistered to smoky sweetness. They are then doused in a spice blend which is rubbed in with lime wedges. We often ate this at home as a healthy snack with chaat masala, a store-bought spice blend that is spicy and sour. I don't have a garden these days so instead of barbecuing my corn, I parboil it, then grill it over an open flame on my gas stove, turning with tongs until it has the right level of char. You can also use a griddle or stovetop grill pan; it should take around 20 minutes.

Delhi-style grilled corn

If you are griddling the corn cobs, or cooking them over a barbecue, do so over medium-low heat, turning often, until the kernels become golden and blister in areas.

Otherwise, place the corn cobs in a pot of boiling water, return to a boil, and cook for eight to 10 minutes. Lift out, place on paper towels, and pat dry. Now place the cobs directly on the flame of a gas stove. Turn with tongs until at least two-thirds of the corn is slightly charred.

However you chose to cook it, now rub one of the lime halves up and down each cob and sprinkle liberally all around with the chaat masala and a little chili powder, if you like the heat. Take the used lime wedge and use it to rub this masala in really well, then serve.

MAKES 4

4 corn cobs, husks and silk removed
2 limes or lemons, halved
4 teaspoons chaat masala, or to taste
chili powder, to taste

My Indian vegetarian BLT! The paneer is broiled in a spicy marinade and lightly charred; the black cardamom adds a smoky dimension. The tangy mayonnaise mixture contains some Greek yogurt for freshness and tang. All in all, this is a warm, spicy, crunchy sandwich that is very addictive. Of course, it will be better if you make your own paneer (see page 9) but, if you use store-bought paneer, steep it in boiling water for 15 minutes to soften before marinating and cooking.

"PLT"

Stir together the yogurt, ginger, garlic, ground spices, lemon juice, and oil and season to taste. Grate in the cardamom (I use a fine Microplane, but a nutmeg grater will work).

Place the paneer in the marinade and leave for at least 20 minutes. Put a piece of foil on a broiler tray and turn the broiler to high. Arrange the paneer slices on the rack and broil for 10 minutes, turning once, or until the edges are charring.

Meanwhile, toast the bread. Stir together the mayo, yogurt, lemon juice, and milk and season lightly.

Spread the mayo over one piece of toast, place over an even layer of tomato slices, then lettuce. Top with the paneer, add the onion slices, then the last toast. Serve immediately.

MAKES 4

FOR THE MARINADE
scant ⅔ cup Greek yogurt
1⅓ teaspoons peeled, grated gingerroot
1 teaspoon grated garlic
1⅓ teaspoons chili powder
1⅓ teaspoons ground cumin
1⅓ teaspoons garam masala
1⅓ teaspoons paprika
8 teaspoons lemon juice
4 tablespoons vegetable oil
salt, to taste
4 black cardamom pods (optional)

FOR THE SANDWICH
11 ounces paneer (preferably homemade,
    see page 9), cut into long ½-inch slices
8 slices of whole wheat or other bread, thin
    or medium sliced
8 teaspoons mayonnaise (can be light)
2 tablespoons Greek yogurt
4 teaspoons lemon juice
4 teaspoons whole milk, plus more if needed
2 small vine tomatoes, finely sliced
a few crisp lettuce leaves
a few finely sliced rounds of red onions,
    separated into rings

A lovely light meal which, despite having a few components, is easy to make and utterly delicious. I often serve this with Warm Puy Lentils (see page 152) or Roasted Spiced Portobello (see page 63). I have used butternut squash here as it's so widely available, but try to find different varieites, such as kabocha or acorn squash, as the contrast of green skin and orange flesh is great.

Spice-roasted butternut squash with tomatoes and capered yogurt

Preheat the oven to 375°F.

Cut the squash into wedges, around 1–1¼ inches thick. I leave the skin on. Grind the cinnamon, cloves, fennel seeds, and star anise to a powder. Stir into the oil with the salt and chili powder. Toss the squash wedges in the spiced oil, place on a roasting tray, and roast for 25 minutes, or until tender to the point of a knife.

While these cook, make the yogurt. Heat the oil for the yogurt, add the capers, and allow them to fry and their moisture to evaporate for two or three minutes. Stir into the yogurt with the sugar, season to taste, and set aside. Wipe the pan.

Heat the oil for the tomatoes, add the panch phoran, reduce the heat, and cook until the seeds stop popping. Add the tomatoes and season well. Cook for two to three minutes over high heat, or just until the tomatoes start to soften.

Serve the squash with the tomatoes and a helping of yogurt.

SERVES 3 TO 4, CAN BE DOUBLED

FOR THE SQUASH
1 pound 2 ounces butternut squash (weight without seeds)
3-inch cinnamon stick
6 cloves
⅔ teaspoon fennel seeds
1 small star anise
1½ tablespoons olive oil
salt, to taste
½–¾ teaspoon chili powder, or to taste

FOR THE CAPERED YOGURT
1 tablespoon olive oil
1½ tablespoons capers, rinsed
1 cup Greek yogurt
1½–1¾ teaspoons superfine sugar, or to taste

FOR THE TOMATOES
1 tablespoon olive oil
1 rounded teaspoon panch phoran, or use equal quantities of cumin, fennel, mustard, and nigella seeds
11 ounces baby tomatoes, halved

The sun did not have to come out in the summer for the barbecue to be lit in our home. If it was forecast to be a warm and rain-free weekend, my parents would start inviting people. I think barbecues are the best way of entertaining in summer if you have a garden or backyard, and are great for getting flavor into vegetables. Here is a lovely, easy marinade to get you started. You can grill any vegetable, this is just a list of those I enjoy with the spicy marinade. Serve with chutneys and lots of salads, such as the Ultimate Kachumber in this photo (see page 155). Definitely put some naans onto grill at the same time (see page 136), as barbecues do wonders for them.

Tandoori vegetable feast

To blanch the vegetables, bring a large pot of salted water to a boil. Throw in each vegetable, separately. Return to a boil, then time the cooking: artichokes and mushrooms take two minutes, cauliflower and asparagus take one. Remove with a slotted spoon and plunge into cold water to stop the cooking. Squeeze mushrooms to remove any excess water. Broccoli, radicchio, fennel, and peppers will not need blanching.

For the marinade, place half the yogurt, the oil, lemon juice, spices, garlic, ginger, and cashews in a blender and blend until smooth. Stir in the remaining yogurt and season generously.

Preheat the broiler to its highest setting, or light the barbecue. Oil a broiler rack or a large baking sheet.

Dip the vegetables in the marinade and coat well. Place on the rack or sheet and barbecue or broil until the paste turns golden and charred in places. Turn and repeat; it takes around 10 minutes in total.

Baste the vegetables with butter and serve with the lemon wedges and Creamy Mint Chutney (see below).

SERVES 4

FOR THE VEGETABLES
salt
1½ pounds vegetables, such as:
  artichoke hearts
  mushrooms
  cauliflower, in large florets
  asparagus spears
  broccoli, in large florets
  purple radicchio or endive, cut into wedges
    through the root
  fennel, cut into ½-inch slices
  bell peppers, quartered lengthwise
a little vegetable oil
2–3 tablespoons melted unsalted butter, to baste
lemon wedges, to serve

FOR THE TANDOORI MARINADE
1¼ cups plain yogurt
3 tablespoons vegetable oil
3 tablespoons lemon juice
3 teaspoons ground cumin
½–¾ teaspoon chili powder, or to taste
1 teaspoon garam masala, or to taste
⅔ teaspoon ground cardamom
4 garlic cloves, peeled and grated
½ ounce gingerroot, peeled weight, grated
⅓ cup cashews, soaked for 10 minutes,
  then drained
good pinch of freshly ground black pepper

Creamy mint chutney
MAKES AROUND 1 CUP

This is the type of chutney, called pudina, that you find in Indian restaurants to eat with your popadums. It's great with tandoori food.
  Blend together 1¼ ounces of mint leaves, 1¼ ounces of cilantro leaves and stalks, 2 teaspoons of roasted ground cumin (see page 9), 1 tablespoon of superfine sugar, 1 green chile, seeded, and scant ¼ cup of yogurt until smooth. Season with salt, then stir in ⅔ cup more yogurt and lemon juice to taste. Adjust the seasoning and serve.

GLORIOUS
VEGETABLES

I absolutely love this. It's a very Punjabi dish known as bharta in India, and it's great with lentil and bean curries, or just with crispy naan or flatbreads and some creamy raita.

Smoky spiced eggplants

Smear the eggplants with a little oil, place directly over a gas flame, and cook, turning often, until charred all over. It will take around 15 minutes. (Or roast them in the oven at 425°F for 25 to 30 minutes.) Sprinkle water all over and let cool.

Meanwhile, heat the ghee in a nonstick pan. Add the onions and chiles and cook until soft. Add the ginger and garlic and cook, stirring, for a minute or so. Add the tomatoes, spices, and salt and cook until the tomatoes release oil back into the pan, stirring occasionally. This should take about 15 minutes.

Meanwhile, peel the skin from the eggplants and discard. Chop the flesh and add it to the tomato pan with any juices that have accumulated in the eggplant dish, then tip in the peas. Cook over medium-low heat, stirring occasionally, for 15 to 20 minutes, until the moisture has dried off and the mixture looks creamy. Cover and let rest for five minutes, then stir in the chopped cilantro and serve.

SERVES 4 GENEROUSLY

2 large eggplants
a little vegetable oil
3 tablespoons ghee (or half oil, half butter)
2 small-ish onions, minced
1–3 green chiles, whole but pierced with the tip of a knife
¾ ounce gingerroot, peeled weight, minced
2 garlic cloves, peeled and minced
4 tomatoes, chopped
2 rounded teaspoons ground coriander
1 teaspoon ground cumin
¾ teaspoon garam masala
salt, to taste
2 large handfuls of green peas (I use frozen)
handful of chopped cilantro leaves

Cucumber and mint raita
SERVES 4

Refreshing and versatile, this is great with grilled food, or just a piece of pita bread.

Grate ½ large cucumber coarsely, squeeze out excess water, and place in a large bowl. Stir in 1¾ cups of yogurt, ¼ ounce of shredded mint leaves, ¾ teaspoon of roasted ground cumin (see page 9), and a small pinch each of superfine sugar and chili powder. Season well, taste, and adjust the seasoning. Refrigerate until ready to use.

This is lovely and creamy but light enough so as to not overpower the vegetables, which stand proud. Korma was created for the Moghul palaces, using the most expensive ingredients of the time: nuts, cream, saffron, and dried fruit. Most of these are no longer so dear, except for saffron, but I do love it and always keep some in the refrigerator (the best place for it). If you don't have any, leave it out, the sauce will be less aromatic but still lovely. I have specified types of vegetables, but you can use almost any; I would only recommend keeping the pepper as it adds a lovely flavor.

Delicate korma with cashews and apricots

Place the onion in a pan and cover with boiling water. Return to a boil and simmer for around 12 minutes, or until soft. Drain. Soak ¼ cup of the cashews and all the almonds in boiling water for 10 minutes. Drain, then peel the almonds. Blend both types of nut with the yogurt, milk, cream, coconut cream, drained onion, saffron, sugar, and ground spices, adding a little water, until you have a smooth paste. Set aside.

Put the cauliflower, pepper, carrot, mushrooms, and beans in a pan and add enough water to come one-quarter of the way up. Season and bring to a boil. Cover and simmer for four minutes, until just soft. Add the peas, cook for 30 seconds, then pour everything, including the cooking liquor, into a bowl.

Give the pan a wipe and place back on the heat. Add the oil and, once hot, the remaining cashews, and cook until golden. Remove and set aside. Add the cumin seeds to the pan. Once they darken, add the chiles, ginger, and garlic, cook gently until the garlic smells cooked, scraping the pan if things start to stick and adding a splash of water if you're worried they might burn. Pour in the blended nut mixture and bring to a boil. Cook for five or six minutes, stirring often.

Return the vegetables with enough of their cooking liquid to give a creamy, but not thick, curry. Season to taste and add the apricots and fried cashews. Taste, adjust the seasoning and sweetness, and serve.

SERVES 4

Tangerine and mint raita
SERVES 4

Lovely and refreshing with the korma.
 Peel and segment 4 tangerines, removing the pithy membranes. Stir into 2½ cups of yogurt and add 12 shredded mint leaves, a pinch of chili powder, 1 teaspoon of superfine sugar, and salt to taste. Taste and adjust the seasoning and sugar, then chill in the refrigerator until you are ready to eat.

FOR THE KORMA

1 small onion, peeled and quartered
⅓ cup cashews
¼ cup almonds
3 rounded tablespoons yogurt
generous ¾ cup whole milk
4 tablespoons heavy cream
1½–2 ounces coconut cream or creamed coconut
15 long saffron strands
1 teaspoon superfine sugar, or to taste
½ teaspoon ground cardamom
½ teaspoon ground cinnamon
1 teaspoon garam masala
2 tablespoons vegetable oil
1½ teaspoons cumin seeds
3–4 green chiles, whole but pierced with the tip of a knife
¾ ounce gingerroot, peeled weight, grated
3 fat garlic cloves, peeled and grated
salt, to taste

FOR THE VEGETABLES (SEE RECIPE INTRODUCTION)

4 ounces cauliflower, in florets
¾–1 small red bell pepper, in 1-inch cubes
1 very small carrot, in ½-inch half moons
3½ ounces oyster or cremini mushrooms (choose small ones)
3 ounces fine beans, trimmed and cut in three
handful of peas (I use frozen)
8 dried, ready-to-eat apricots, halved if small or quartered if large

This is a taste experience that I highly recommend. Juhu Beach is a famous stretch of sand in Mumbai. I haven't been for decades, but I remember it to be as bustling as any busy street: a throng of people to maneuvre around, pony rides for children, blaring Bollywood music, a monotonous cacophony of hawkers ... and the tempting smell of food. Pau bhaji just means bread and vegetables, but that name does no justice to this glorious recipe. It is a divine, buttery Indian vegetable mash with a thick spongy bread crisped up in butter, served with lemon wedges and red onion. You will need to buy pau bhaji masala, but this is easily available online and is a really versatile spice blend.

Juhu Beach pau bhaji

Place the pepper and cauliflower in a large, wide pan. Place on the heat, add enough water to come ½ inch up the pan, bring to a boil, then reduce the heat and simmer for five minutes. Add some salt, the tomatoes, potatoes, tomato paste, paprika, 2 teaspoons of the pau bhaji masala, the cilantro, peas, and generous ⅓ cup of the butter.

Now you have to cook this mixture, adding water when the pan is dry. As it cooks, you need to keep mashing the whole thing (I use a potato masher) until it is all cooked and has become a lumpy puree. It will take around 30 minutes and you will keep needing to add water when it starts to catch the bottom of the pan. Taste; it should all seem harmonious and cooked and look lovely and creamy and mashed. Leave it on low heat as you cook the onion.

Heat the remaining butter with the oil for the tarka in a small pan, add the onion, and cook until just soft, then add the garlic and ginger and cook until the garlic is lightly golden. Add another 1 teaspoon of the pau bhaji masala and give it another 30 seconds, add the cilantro, then pour into the vegetables. Add lemon juice to taste and a little splash of water and cook for another five minutes. Taste, adding more of the masala if you think it needs it, then adjust the seasoning and lemon juice to taste.

When ready to eat, slice the pau or burger buns in half and spread with butter. Place butter-side down in a skillet and toast lightly, pressing down so it gets crispy and golden in places.

Serve the bread hot with the vegetables, a little bowl of minced onion and the lemon wedges. Take a piece of the bread, top with some of the vegetable mixture, sprinkle over a little onion, and squeeze over lemon juice to taste.

SERVES 6, CAN BE HALVED

FOR THE VEGETABLES
1 small green bell pepper, in roughly
    ½-inch cubes
11 ounces cauliflower, in small florets
salt, to taste
3 large tomatoes, chopped
2 large potatoes (1 pound 2 ounces total
    weight), cooked, peeled, and roughly cubed
1 tablespoon tomato paste
2 teaspoons paprika, for color
3–4 teaspoons pau bhaji masala, to taste
large handful of cilantro leaves,
    plus more to serve
large handful of peas (I use frozen)
½–scant ¾ cup unsalted butter, plus more for
    the bread (it is supposed to be buttery)
4 teaspoons lemon juice, or to taste

FOR THE TARKA
1 teaspoon vegetable oil
1 small onion, minced
4 fat garlic cloves, peeled and grated
¾ ounce gingerroot, peeled weight, grated
small handful of chopped cilantro leaves

TO SERVE
8 pau or white burger buns
1 red onion, minced
lemon wedges

Okra is a much misunderstood vegetable. Many people consider them uninteresting. But they can have a lovely texture, are flavorful, and healthy. To avoid any sliminess, the okra are cooked in a skillet away from any liquid, then added to a lightly spiced, tangy sauce. Keeping the okra intact will maintain their character and flavor. Serve with a creamy, flavorful raita (see below).

Spiced okra in tomato sauce

Heat 4 tablespoons of the vegetable oil in a nonstick pan. Add the cumin, fennel, and onion seeds and cook for 10 to 15 seconds, or until the cumin is aromatic. Add the onions and cook until just coloring on the edges.

Meanwhile, blend together the tomatoes and yogurt until smooth. Add to the onions with the remaining spices and some salt. Bring to a boil then simmer, stirring occasionally, until the sauce is thick and has released some oil back into the pan. Continue cooking, stirring more often, for another two to three minutes. Add generous ¾ cup of water, return to a boil, then reduce the heat and simmer gently.

Meanwhile, heat the remaining oil in a large nonstick skillet. Add the okra and a little salt and cook, shaking the skillet every now and then, for five to seven minutes, or until the okra are just soft. Add to the sauce, stir well, taste, and adjust the seasoning, then simmer for another minute and serve.

SERVES 4

5 tablespoons vegetable oil
½ teaspoon cumin seeds
½ teaspoon fennel seeds
½ teaspoon onion seeds
2 small onions, minced
2 tomatoes, quartered
2 tablespoons yogurt
⅓ teaspoon turmeric
¾ teaspoon garam masala
1½ teaspoons ground coriander
¾ teaspoon ground cumin
¼–½ teaspoon chili powder
salt, to taste
11 ounces okra, trimmed, each slit down its
   length

Carrot, cucumber, and peanut raita
SERVES 4

Nutty, crunchy, and lovely.

   Lightly salt 5 ounces of coarsely grated cucumber, leave for 10 minutes, squeeze out excess water, and place in a bowl. Add 1 large carrot, also coarsely grated, 3 tablespoons of chopped cilantro leaves, 1½ heaping tablespoons of roasted peanuts, coarsely crushed, and ½ minced chile. Now stir in generous 1 cup of thick yogurt, season to taste, adding 1 teaspoon of superfine sugar and 2 tablespoons of grated fresh coconut, if you like. Heat 1 teaspoon of vegetable oil in a small pan, add ½ teaspoon of mustard seeds and, when the popping dies down, 6 or 7 curry leaves. Cook for another 10 seconds, then stir into the yogurt. Taste, adjust the seasoning, and serve.

This is a typical Keralan curry, lighter in flavor and fresher than a North Indian curry, and quicker to make because of it. This is a great base sauce to which you can add many different vegetables: try eggplants, okra, spinach, broccoli, peas, mushrooms, chickpeas, green beans, and pumpkin or squash. If you like fruity curries, some pineapple, bell peppers, and peanuts would also be lovely (you will need to use less tamarind and perhaps add a pinch of sugar). Here I have used sweet potatoes, chickpeas, and seasonal greens. Serve with rice, naan, or parathas.

Keralan coconut curry

Put the sweet potatoes onto boil and cook until just done; it should take around 10 minutes.

Heat the oil in a large nonstick pan and add the mustard seeds. Once the popping diminishes, add the onion and green chilies and sauté for two to three minutes or until just softening, then add the ginger and garlic; sauté these gently for one minute. Add the tomatoes, salt, turmeric, and ground coriander and cumin and keep sautéing for four to five minutes. Now taste; it should seem harmonious and the tomatoes should be soft but still retain their form.

Add the coconut milk and a splash of water. Bring to a gentle simmer and cook for five to seven minutes. At this point I take out the chiles as I might mistake them for spinach and inadvertently bite into one but, if you aren't using green vegetables, leave them in. Add the greens and cook for a few minutes, then add the drained sweet potatoes, the chickpeas, most of the tamarind, the garam masala, and the coconut cream. Taste, adjust the seasoning, adding more tamarind to taste, and serve.

SERVES 4

FOR THE VEGETABLES (SEE RECIPE INTRODUCTION FOR OTHER OPTIONS)
14 ounces sweet potatoes, peeled, in 1¼-inch chunks
generous 1 cup shredded greens or spinach, washed
14-ounce can chickpeas, drained and rinsed

FOR THE CURRY
4 tablespoons vegetable oil
1 teaspoon mustard seeds
1 onion, minced
3–5 green chiles, whole but pierced with the tip of a knife
1 ounce gingerroot, peeled weight, minced
5 fat garlic cloves, peeled and minced
2 small tomatoes, chopped
salt, to taste
½–⅔ teaspoon turmeric
2 teaspoons ground coriander
¾–1 teaspoon ground cumin
1¾ cups creamy coconut milk
½–¾ teaspoon tamarind paste, dissolved in a little hot water, to taste
¾ teaspoon garam masala, or to taste
little piece of coconut cream
lots of freshly ground pepper

Rogan josh is a world-famous lamb dish from Kashmir, but has morphed quite a bit along the way ... always remaining spicy, rich, and very flavorful. Kashmiri dried chiles are known for the deep red color and are mild. I serve this with Spinach and Dill Raita (see below), naan, or flatbreads.

Rogan mushrooms

Roast the dried chiles in a dry pan until slightly darkened, shaking often. Break in half and shake out the seeds, then grind to a powder. Heat 4 tablespoons of the oil in a large nonstick pan. Add the whole spices and fry for 10 seconds. Add the onions and cook until they have browned well at the edges.

Meanwhile, blend together the tomatoes, yogurt, garlic, and ginger until smooth. Add to the onions with the ground spices and some salt. Cook, stirring occasionally, until the masala has completely reduced and releases oil droplets back into the pan. Continue to cook, stirring often, over highish heat, for four to five minutes. Add 1½ cups of water, bring to a boil, simmer for three to four minutes, then keep warm.

Heat 1 tablespoon of the remaining oil and half the butter in a large skillet. Add half the mushrooms, sprinkle over a pinch of salt, and sauté, allowing them to caramelize on the edges, for around five minutes. Repeat with the remaining oil, butter, and mushrooms. As they are ready, pour the mushrooms into the sauce and stir well, then taste and adjust the seasoning. Add a little water if necessary; the sauce should be thick but not too clingy. Simmer for another three to four minutes then serve, sprinkled with the chopped cilantro.

SERVES 4

2–4 dried red Kashmiri chiles (see recipe introduction)
6 tablespoons vegetable oil
4 cloves
6 green cardamom pods
2 black cardamom pods
2-inch cinnamon stick
1 mace blade
10 black peppercorns
2 small onions, minced
2 large tomatoes, quartered
2 rounded tablespoons yogurt
5 garlic cloves, peeled
¾ ounce gingerroot, peeled weight
2 teaspoons ground coriander
¾ teaspoon ground cumin
⅓ teaspoon turmeric
¾ teaspoon garam masala, or to taste
salt, to taste
2 heaping tablespoons unsalted butter
12 ounces assorted mushrooms (I use shiitake, cremini, and oyster), halved if large
handful of chopped cilantro leaves

Spinach and dill raita
SERVES 4

This is silky and delicious and, somehow, children love it!
Wilt 3 ounces of baby spinach in a pan. Drain and squeeze out the excess water with your hands. Stir into 1¼ cups of yogurt, season, and add ¾ teaspoon of roasted ground cumin (see page 9) and 2 teaspoons of dill fronds, chopped. Serve chilled.

This is a classic Sindhi dish called sai bhaji. It was taught to me by my good friend Shaila and is her mother-in-law's recipe. It is so delicious that I don't think I have made a single change, which is a first! It is a proper stew, full of vegetables and so healthy, no wonder mothers insist on passing it onto their children. This is not a party dish, but one which you will cook for your family again and again; it is hearty and tangy and perfect with both Indian flatbreads and rice.

Lemony spinach and vegetable hotchpotch

Using a stick blender, blend together the ginger and garlic with a little water until smooth. Set aside. Again using the stick blender, blend the tomatoes until smooth. Set these aside as well.

Heat the oil in a large nonstick pan. Add the onion and cook until just soft. Add the blended ginger and garlic and cook until the liquid has dried up and the garlic turns lightly golden. Add the tomatoes, spices, and salt and bring to a boil; simmer for five minutes.

Add the carrot, eggplant, and potato and give the pan a good stir. Sprinkle over the drained lentils, but do not stir them in. Place the spinach, herbs, and fenugreek on top and pour in generous ¾ cup of water. Without stirring the pan, bring to a boil, then cover and simmer on gentle heat until yieldingly soft, around 1 to 1¼ hours.

Uncover and, if you like, mash the vegetables and spinach together until homogeneous (this is how the authentic recipe is made; I prefer to leave the vegetables whole). Add the lemon juice to taste and adjust the seasoning. Simmer off any excess water as the stew cooks for another 15 minutes and becomes creamy, then serve.

SERVES 5 TO 6

¾ ounce gingerroot, peeled weight
3 fat garlic cloves, peeled
4 large tomatoes, quartered
3 tablespoons vegetable oil
1 large onion, chopped
2 rounded teaspoons ground cumin
1 tablespoon ground coriander
½ teaspoon turmeric
1 rounded teaspoon garam masala
salt, to taste
1 large-ish carrot, peeled and chopped into ¾-ounce pieces
½ large eggplant, cut into ¾-inch pieces
1 potato, peeled and cut into ¾-inch pieces
4 tablespoons Bengal gram (chana dal), soaked for two hours, or as long as possible
1 pound 2 ounces baby spinach, washed
½ tablespoon dill fronds or 1 ounce cilantro leaves, roughly chopped
1 tablespoon dried fenugreek leaves, crumbled between your fingers
1–1½ tablespoons lemon juice

This is based on a vegetarian national treasure, mirch salan, a Hyderabadi dish of fat, large green chiles in a peanut and tamarind sauce. The combination is fabulous. But I recently came across these lovely mixed baby sweet peppers at my local supermarket and decided they would be great in the dish. If you like a little more heat, find large, fat, jalapeño-type chiles and follow the recipe below, except add them to the sauce and simmer for a few minutes at the end. It is definitely a special occasion dish, but is fun to make and well worth it. The sauce also goes well with mushrooms, eggplants, okra, and many other vegetables. I like to have some naan on the side to mop up all those lovely flavors.

Stuffed peppers in a peanut-tamarind sauce

Dry-roast the peanuts in a small skillet for a minute and pour into a spice grinder. Add the sesame and cumin seeds to the skillet and dry-roast gently until the sesame is golden. Pour into the spice grinder with the coconut and grind to a powder; don't worry about any chunks.

Heat 4 tablespoons of the oil in a pan and add the onions; sauté until golden. Meanwhile, with a stick blender, blend the ginger and garlic with a little water until smooth. Separately, blend the tomatoes until smooth. Add the ginger and garlic to the onions and sauté until the garlic colors. Add the tomatoes, ground spices, and salt. Bring to a boil and cook for 10 to 15 minutes, until the masala releases oil back into the pan. Brown this paste, over highish heat, for three to four minutes, then stir in the ground nut mixture. Add 1¾ cups of water, return to a boil, and simmer for eight minutes. Add most of the tamarind, then adjust the seasoning and tamarind. It should be a slightly chunky, creamy curry, neither watery nor too thick.

For the stuffing, heat 1 tablespoon of the remaining oil in a large nonstick skillet. Add the onion and cook until soft, add the turmeric and, after a beat, the potato, cumin, and salt to taste; cook for two minutes. Add the lemon juice, mix, adjust the seasoning, and place in a bowl to cool. Give it a good mash if it is lumpy. Wipe the pan. Slit the peppers lengthwise so you can open them, then stuff them. Do not overstuff.

Cook the peppers in two batches: in 1 tablespoon of the remaining oil for each batch, add half the mustard seeds, and reduce the heat. Once the popping dies down, add half the curry leaves and peppers. Stir for 20 seconds and season lightly. Then add a splash of hot water, cover, and steam for 10 minutes or until the peppers are soft; they will have lightly charred in places. Shake gently every so often. Keep warm while you repeat with the next batch.

Place the peppers on warmed plates. Spoon the sauce over and sprinkle with coconut, or peanuts and chopped cilantro. Serve hot.

SERVES 6

½ cup raw peanuts, skins rubbed off if there are any, plus more to serve (optional)
2 tablespoons sesame seeds
1 tablespoon cumin seeds
1 rounded tablespoon dry unsweetened coconut, plus more to serve (optional)
7 tablespoons vegetable oil
2 onions, minced
3/4 ounce gingerroot, peeled weight
4 large garlic cloves, peeled
2 tomatoes, quartered
1 rounded tablespoon ground coriander
1½ teaspoons garam masala
½ teaspoon turmeric
¼–½ teaspoon chili powder, or to taste
salt, to taste
½–¾ teaspoon tamarind paste, dissolved in 3 tablespoons boiling water, or to taste
12 baby mixed peppers
¾ teaspoon mustard seeds
10 curry leaves
small fistful of chopped cilantro leaves, to serve (optional)

FOR THE STUFFING
½ onion, minced
²/₃ teaspoon turmeric
1 pound potatoes, boiled or microwaved, peeled, and coarsely mashed
1 rounded teaspoon cumin seeds
1½–2 teaspoons lemon juice

I don't know anyone who doesn't love a pie; they are comforting and homey and also special enough for when you have friends around. This pie doesn't need any more than a salad on the side. I love the rustic cobbler topping, it is really quick and simple, but you can also cover the pie with puff pastry if you prefer. You can serve this in a large dish, or individual dishes. I roast the squash here rather than cooking it in the curry, only because it is easier than cutting raw squash into pieces!

Fall squash, lima bean, and mushroom cobbler

Preheat the oven to 400°F. Halve the squash, remove any fibers and seeds, but leave the skin on. Place it in a roasting pan and cook until soft, around 30 minutes. Cut into 1-inch squares, removing the skin if you want.

Meanwhile, heat the oil in a large pan until hot. Add the onion and cook until soft and coloring at the edges. Add the ginger and garlic and cook until the garlic just starts to color. Add the tomatoes, spices, and seasoning and cook down until the sauce has thickened and has released oil back into the pan.

Add the mushrooms, cover, and cook for another two to three minutes. Pour in generous ¾ cup of water and add the beans, squash, and spinach and return to a boil. Cook for two to three minutes. Add the cream and milk, taste—making sure you taste both squash and sauce—and adjust the seasoning. Stir in the tomato paste if you feel the tomatoes are lacking flavor or color. By now the sauce should be thick and cling to the vegetables. Spoon into a large pie dish, or six individual dishes.

Make the cobbler topping. Place the flour and salt in a large bowl, add the butter, and rub between your fingers until you have a sandy texture. Make a well in the middle, add half the egg and most of the milk, and bring together with a fork to a very soft dough. Turn out onto a flour-dusted counter and lightly bring together. Pat out until it is about ½ inch thick and, using a cookie cutter, cut out six circles. (I use large cutters and make the circles big enough to cover the filling with just a little showing at the sides.)

Place the cobbler circles on the pie filling, brush with the remaining beaten egg, sprinkle over some sea salt, and bake on the middle shelf of the oven until the cobbler topping has turned a lovely deep golden brown, 20 to 25 minutes. Serve.

SERVES 5 TO 6

FOR THE PIE FILLING

14 ounces squash (I like butternut, hubbard, or acorn)
4 tablespoons vegetable oil
1 onion, chopped
¾ ounce gingerroot, peeled weight, grated
3 large garlic cloves, peeled and grated
3 tomatoes, quartered
¾ teaspoon turmeric
½–1 teaspoon chili powder
2 teaspoons ground coriander
½ teaspoon garam masala
salt, to taste
good pinch of freshly ground black pepper
9–10 large cremini mushrooms, thickly sliced
14-ounce can lima beans, drained and rinsed
3½ ounces baby spinach
6 tablespoons heavy cream
scant ¼ cup whole milk
½–1 tablespoon tomato paste (optional)

FOR THE COBBLER TOPPING

1¼ cups self-rising flour, sifted, plus more to dust
⅓ teaspoon salt
scant ⅓ cup unsalted butter, cut into smallish pieces
2 eggs, beaten
scant ¼–generous ¼ cup whole milk
a few sea salt flakes

I love corn in most guises, but few dishes are as delicious as this. The cobs are enrobed in a tangy, tomato-based curry laced with crushed roasted peanuts, adding texture and flavor. The result is absolutely delicious and the dish easy to make. I normally eat the cobs with my fingers and mop up the sauce with Indian breads but, if that feels awkward, use corn kernels instead of cobs and eat the dish with a knife and fork.

Corn cobs in tangy peanut masala

Heat the oil in a large nonstick pan. Add the cumin seeds, follow with the onion, and sauté until golden.

Meanwhile, blend together the tomatoes, ginger, and garlic until smooth. Add to the onion with the ground spices. Cook until the masala has completely reduced and released oil back into the pan. Stir-fry for three to four minutes to intensify the flavors.

Meanwhile, bring a large pot of water to a boil and add your corn cobs. Return to a boil and cook for 10 minutes, or until the kernels are just tender. Drain and, when cool enough to handle, cut each cob into four with a heavy knife (be very careful).

Returning to the masala, add the peanuts with 2½ cups of water and bring to a boil, then reduce the heat and simmer for five minutes. Add the corn cobs, cover, and simmer for another five to seven minutes or until the sauce has thickened and there is a little oil on the surface.

Taste and adjust the seasoning, adding cilantro leaves and lemon juice to taste. The sauce will taste different when eaten with the corn so, if you are not sure, serve the dish with lemon wedges on the side.

SERVES 4

4 tablespoons vegetable oil
1½ teaspoons cumin seeds
1 red onion, minced
5 tomatoes
¾ ounce gingerroot, peeled weight
4 large garlic cloves, peeled
2 rounded teaspoons ground coriander
⅓ teaspoon turmeric
1½ teaspoons garam masala
¾ teaspoon chili powder, to taste
4 small corn cobs
1 cup roasted peanuts, coarsely crushed
salt, to taste
handful of cilantro leaves
lemon juice, to taste (I add around 1–1½ tablespoons because I like the tang), plus lemon wedges to serve (optional)

This is a tomato-based curry where the vegetables take center stage, retaining their own textures and flavors. You really can make a jhalfrezi with any vegetables as long as you use the same volume; I have listed a few options just to give you some ideas. Look for a good mix of colors, shapes, and textures. If you can find baby vegetables, it will make this even more special. Only use pomegranate seeds if they are ripe, otherwise they add too much sourness. I like this quite spicy, so I add crushed chiles at the end, but I leave that up to you and your palate. Serve with naan.

Vegetable jhalfrezi with pomegranates

Using a stick blender, blend the tomatoes until smooth. Heat the oil in a large nonstick pan. Add the grated ginger and garlic and cook, stirring often, until the garlic is cooked and starts to color, around one minute. Add the green chiles, tomatoes, ground coriander, garam masala, and salt. Bring to a boil and let simmer until the tomatoes have completely reduced and the sauce releases oil on the bottom of the pan. Taste; it should seem harmonious.

Meanwhile, cook your chosen vegetables. Bring a pot of water to a boil and salt lightly. Add your vegetables in order of how long they take to cook. I add the starchier vegetables first (here the potatoes, carrots, and squash), then follow five minutes later with the eggplants and zucchini, then one to two minutes later with the beans and peas. Cook until they are ready, another two minutes or so. Check as you cook. Drain, but set the cooking water aside.

When ready to serve, add the red bell pepper strips, ginger julienne, fenugreek leaves, and ⅔ cup of the vegetable cooking liquor to the sauce and return to a boil. Taste and adjust the seasoning, adding the crushed chile, if using. Add the vegetables and stir well to coat them in the light tomato sauce. Splash in a little water if the sauce is too thick; it should be of coating consistency. Ladle into a warmed serving dish, spoon over the cream in a circular pattern, sprinkle the pomegranate powder over the cream so you can see it, and then do the same with the pomegranate seeds, if using. Serve.

SERVES 4

FOR THE SAUCE
2 large ripe tomatoes, quartered
5 tablespoons vegetable oil, or a mix of unsalted butter and oil
½ ounce gingerroot, peeled weight, half grated, half sliced into fine julienne
4 fat garlic cloves, peeled and grated
4–5 green chiles, whole but pierced with the tip of a knife
2 rounded teaspoons ground coriander
1 teaspoon garam masala
salt, to taste
½ small red bell pepper, finely sliced
2 teaspoons dried fenugreek leaves, crushed
¼ teaspoon crushed red chiles (optional)
2 tablespoons light cream (optional)
good pinch of dried pomegranate powder (optional)
handful of pomegranate seeds (optional)

FOR THE VEGETABLES (YOU NEED 3 HANDFULS OF PREPARED VEGETABLES)
fingerling or baby potatoes, cooked, peeled, then halved or quartered lengthwise
carrots or parsnips, peeled, halved lengthwise, then sliced at an angle
wedge of butternut squash or pumpkin, peeled, cut into wedges
Japanese eggplants, quartered lengthwise (leave the stalk on)
zucchini, sliced at an angle
fava beans, sugar snap peas, green beans, or snow peas (all trimmed, and green beans halved)

This is a lovely delicate, pale curry where you can taste all the vegetables but also the delicate mint and pistachios. You can use whichever vegetables you prefer, these are just a few I like to use. I tend to cook my vegetables before adding them to a sauce, so both sauce and vegetables retain their own characters. Serve with naan, paratha, or a pilaf.

Creamy pistachio curry

Bring a pot of water to a boil and salt lightly. Add your vegetables in order of how long they take to cook. I add the starchier vegetables first (here the squash), then follow five minutes later with the cauliflower, then one to two minutes later with the broccoli and snow peas. Cook until they are ready, another two minutes or so. Check as you cook. Drain, but set the cooking water aside.

Meanwhile, soak the pistachios for five minutes in boiling water Remove the skins; they peel off easily when rubbed in a clean dish towel. Roughly chop one-third of the nuts. Blend together the rest of the pistachios until smooth, adding a little water to help.

Heat the oil in a large nonstick pan; add the cloves, cardamom, cassia, and caraway seeds. Follow after 20 seconds with the onion and green chiles and cook until the onion is golden on the edges. Add the ginger and garlic and sauté gently for one to two minutes, or until the garlic is just golden.

Add the ground cumin and coriander and the yogurt and bring to a boil, stirring constantly. Continue to cook, stirring, until the masala thickens and releases oil back into the pan, around five to eight minutes. Taste; it should seem harmonious. If not, cook for another couple of minutes.

Add the blanched vegetables, some of their cooking water, the pepper, cream, and both blended and chopped pistachios. Cook for another two or three minutes for everything to come together. The sauce should be creamy and not too thick, so add water if necessary. Check the seasoning, adjust as necessary, crumble over the dried mint, then serve.

SERVES 4

FOR THE VEGETABLES (AROUND 12 OUNCES, USE WHICHEVER YOU PREFER)
salt
3½ ounces butternut squash, cut into 1¼–1½-inch cubes (or sweet potato or carrots)
3½ ounces cauliflower, cut into 1¼–1½-inch florets
3½ ounces broccoli, cut into 1¼–1½-inch florets
2 ounces snow peas, trimmed (or other beans or peas)

FOR THE CURRY
scant ½ cup pistachios
4 tablespoons vegetable oil
6 cloves
6 green cardamom pods
2-inch cassia bark or cinnamon stick
1 teaspoon caraway seeds
1 small-ish onion, minced
1–2 green chiles, whole but pierced with the tip of a knife
¾ ounce gingerroot, peeled weight, grated
4 fat garlic cloves, peeled and grated
1¼ teaspoons ground cumin
2 teaspoons ground coriander
5 tablespoons yogurt
large pinch of freshly ground black pepper
5 tablespoons light cream
1 tablespoon good-quality dried mint, crumbled between your fingers, or to taste

CHEESE, BEANS,
AND EGGS

Dhansak is a fantastic dish from the Parsi community, made from lentils and vegetables. If you are a fan of dhansak, it might be worth buying the ready-made masala available in most Indian stores (even Parsis use it), though I've given my own recipe here (see below). I like to serve this with simple basmati rice. The traditional vegetables used are pumpkin, eggplant, and potatoes, but I often add other seasonal greens for a one-pot meal (blanch green vegetables before using). Starchy vegetables such as sweet potato, turnips, and so on can be added straight to the lentils.

Parsi dhansak

Place the pigeon peas and both types of lentil in a bowl and wash in several changes of water, until the water runs clear.

Heat the oil in a large pan. Add the onion and sauté until just browned on the edges. Add the ginger and garlic and sauté gently for one to two minutes. Add the lentils, tomato, salt, and turmeric and stir for a few minutes. Pour in enough water to cover by 2 inches and bring to a boil, then reduce the heat, cover, and simmer for 25 to 30 minutes, or until the lentils are soft. Stir occasionally, as the lentils will settle on the bottom of the pan, and add water from the kettle as necessary.

Blend until smooth (I plunge my stick blender into the pot). Add the vegetables with a good splash of water and cook for five minutes. Now add the tamarind, sugar, dhansak masala, and fenugreek and cook for another five minutes, or until the vegetables are just soft. Taste, adjust the seasoning, sugar, and tamarind, stir in the cilantro, and serve.

SERVES 4 TO 6, CAN BE HALVED

½ cup split pigeon peas (toor dal)
¼ cup red lentils (masoor dal)
¼ cup yellow lentils (mung dal)
4 tablespoons vegetable oil
1 onion, sliced
½ ounce gingerroot, peeled weight, roughly sliced
4 fat garlic cloves, peeled and roughly sliced
1 tomato, roughly chopped
salt, to taste
⅓ teaspoon turmeric
¾–1 teaspoon tamarind paste, dissolved in a little water, or to taste
2–2½ teaspoons superfine sugar, or to taste
4 tablespoons My Dhansak Masala (see below left), or to taste
2 teaspoons dried fenugreek leaves, crushed between your fingers
large handful of chopped cilantro leaves

VEGETABLES I HAVE USED (FOR OTHER OPTIONS SEE ABOVE):
4 ounces squash or sweet potatoes, in 1-inch cubes
4 ounces Japanese eggplants, trimmed and cut across into halves or thirds

My dhansak masala

Place 2 tablespoons of coriander seeds, ½-inch of cinnamon stick, 3 cloves, and 1 star anise in a dry skillet and place over medium heat, shaking to brown the spices evenly. After 30 seconds, add 1½ teaspoons of cumin seeds and ½ teaspoon each of caraway, mustard, and fenugreek seeds and roast, shaking the pan often, until the fenugreek and cumin seeds darken, another 30 to 40 seconds or so. Tip into a spice or coffee grinder, add 8 black peppercorns, ¼ teaspoon of freshly grated nutmeg and 1–2 dried chiles. Grind until smooth. Store in a jar in a cool, dark place. This should make enough for the recipe above, allowing for more to be added if you want it.

The lentil curry I eat more than any other. You won't find it on restaurant menus—it is lighter and thinner than the familiar versions—but you can taste the lentils and all the other flavors. I eat it with Indian flatbread and a simple, dry vegetable dish. You can also fry the onions, ginger, garlic, and tomatoes in oil instead of adding them straight to the lentils, but I like it this way.

Easy everyday lentil curry

Place both types of lentil in a bowl and wash in several changes of water, until the water runs clear. Now place them in a large pan with water to cover by 2 inches and bring to a boil. Skim the surface of any scum. Add the onion, ginger, garlic, chiles, tomatoes, turmeric, and seasoning. Return to a boil, reduce the heat, then simmer, partially covered, until the lentils are cooked and the curry starts to look homogeneous, around 40 minutes.

Heat the ghee or butter in a very small pan and let it pool on one side. Add the cumin seeds and asafetida. Once the seeds darken, add the garam masala and ground coriander and take off the heat. Pour into the lentils, add the chopped cilantro, and serve.

SERVES 4

scant ⅔ cup yellow lentils (mung dal),
   washed well
generous ⅓ cup red lentils (masoor dal),
   washed well
½ onion, minced
⅓ ounce gingerroot, peeled weight, minced
2 garlic cloves, peeled and minced
2–4 green chiles, whole but pierced with the
   tip of a knife
2 tomatoes, chopped
½ teaspoon turmeric
salt, to taste
1½–2 tablespoons ghee or unsalted butter
2 rounded teaspoons cumin seeds
⅛ teaspoon, or a small pinch, asafetida
½ teaspoon garam masala
¾ teaspoon ground coriander
handful of chopped cilantro leaves

A classic North Indian dish, this can be dramatic looking, as the yellow lentils stand out from the smaller black beans. Most importantly, it is luscious and delicious. Once the lentils soften, the more you stir them the creamier they become. Lentils and butter go really well together, so I do recommend you add a little butter at the end before serving. This is great with rice or Indian breads.

Bengal tiger lentil curry

Using a stick blender, blend the ¼-ounce chunk of ginger and the garlic with a little water until smooth. Separately blend the tomatoes until smooth. Set both aside. Place both types of lentil in a bowl and wash in several changes of water, until the water runs clear. Now tip them into a large pot, pour in enough water to cover by 3 inches, and bring to a boil. Skim any scum from the surface. Add the turmeric and some salt. Cook, partially covered, giving an occasional stir, until the lentils have softened and are starting to look homogeneous with the water. (Stir more often as they become tender.)

After about 40 minutes, start to make the tarka, but remember to keep giving the lentils a stir. Heat the oil or ghee in a small nonstick pan. Add the cumin seeds and, once they sizzle and darken, add the onion and cook until coloring at the edges. Add the ginger and garlic paste and cook until the extra moisture has evaporated and the garlic is starting to color. Add the tomatoes and remaining ground spices and cook down for 10 to 15 minutes, until the masala releases oil.

Pour the tarka into the lentils with the ginger julienne, adding water from the kettle if it seems too thick. Make sure the whole thing looks like a lovely unctuous mass (if not, cook a little longer, adding water if necessary) then taste and adjust the seasoning. Stir in the chopped cilantro and butter, if using, and serve.

SERVES 4 TO 5

¾ ounce gingerroot, peeled weight, half of it sliced into fine julienne
4 garlic cloves, peeled
4 small-ish tomatoes, quartered
scant 1 cup Bengal gram (chana dal)
generous ⅓ cup split black gram (dhuli hui ma dal)
½ teaspoon turmeric
salt, to taste
4 tablespoons vegetable oil, or half oil, half ghee
2 teaspoons cumin seeds
1 large-ish onion, minced
2 teaspoons ground coriander
1 teaspoon ground cumin
¾ teaspoon garam masala
¼–½ teaspoon chili powder
handful of chopped cilantro leaves
2–4 teaspoons unsalted butter, to serve (optional, see recipe introduction)

The vegetarian version of the much-loved chicken dish, this is absolutely delicious, with a wonderful creamy tomato sauce and a few key spices that work beautifully with the paneer. It is definitely for special occasions, as it has a few steps and is unapologetically creamy. Before you serve it up, please take a minute to balance your sauce for sweetness and tartness, which will vary with the tomatoes. Adjust and taste until you are happy with the balance. Serve with naan or paratha.

Paneer tikka masala

Blend together the ingredients for the tikka marinade until smooth, scrape into a bowl, add the paneer, and stir to coat.

With a stick blender, blend the tomatoes until smooth. Heat the oil and half the butter in a large nonstick pan. Add the whole spices and cook for 10 seconds before adding the ginger and garlic; cook gently until starting to color. Add the tomatoes and tomato paste and cook down until the resulting paste releases oil, around 20 minutes. Now, over medium-low heat, "brown" this paste, stirring often, until it darkens considerably, around eight to 10 minutes. Add generous 1 cup of water, bring to a boil, then pass through a strainer, pressing down on the solids with the back of a spoon until all you have left are fiber and spices; throw these away.

Heat the broiler on its highest setting. Place the paneer on a foil-lined tray and broil for eight to 10 minutes, turning once, or until the edges are lightly charred. Remove from the oven.

Heat the remaining butter and add the green chiles. Add the tomato sauce, powdered spices, salt, sugar, and a good splash of water and simmer for two or three minutes. Add the paneer and simmer for another five to six minutes. Add the cream and simmer, shaking the pan gently, until the sauce is lovely and creamy, around two or three minutes. You may need to add a little more water to get the consistency of light cream. Taste and adjust the balance by adding more salt, sugar, or cream as necessary (cream will lessen any overt acidity from under-ripe tomatoes). Serve and wait for the applause.

SERVES 4 TO 6

FOR THE TIKKA MARINADE
⅓ ounce gingerroot, peeled weight
2 fat garlic cloves, peeled
2 tablespoons lemon juice
⅔ cup Greek yogurt
1 rounded teaspoon chili powder
1 rounded teaspoon ground cumin
1 rounded teaspoon garam masala
1 rounded teaspoon paprika
salt, to taste
3 tablespoons vegetable oil

FOR THE REST
14 ounces paneer (preferably homemade, see page 9), in 1¼–1½-inch cubes
1 pound 2 ounces vine tomatoes, quartered
1 tablespoon vegetable oil
¼ cup (½ stick) unsalted butter
1 black cardamom pod
6 green cardamom pods
2-inch cinnamon stick
4 cloves
¾-ounce gingerroot, peeled weight, grated
4 garlic cloves, grated
1 tablespoon tomato paste
2–4 small green chiles, whole but pierced with the tip of a knife
½ teaspoon garam masala
1 teaspoon paprika, or enough for good color
1½ rounded teaspoons dried fenugreek leaves, crushed with your fingers
salt, to taste
1¼–1½ tablespoons superfine sugar, to taste
¼–generous ⅓ cup light cream, or to taste

I was introduced to this delicious sweet-and-sour lentil dish at a friend's house in Mumbai. It quickly became a firm favorite and they made it for me every trip. Here, I have added dumplings with a vibrant pea and coconut filling to freshen the lentils and make it more elegant, but you can leave them out and just add some diamond-shaped pieces of roti to the lentils, or even leave the lentils as they are. This quite soupy dish is normally served as a stand-alone meal. Cocum is a fruit that grows on tropical trees in parts of India; the dark purple flesh is dried. It adds a lovely sourness and tastes absolutely delicious. If you don't have any, balance the sourness to taste with the tamarind.

Green pea and coconut dumplings in Gujarati lentil curry

Put the pigeon peas in a pan and pour in enough water to cover by 2 inches. Bring to a boil, then add salt and the turmeric and cook, partially covered, for 30 minutes, or until soft, skimming any scum from the surface. Using a stick blender, blend to a smooth puree.

Meanwhile, mix all the ingredients for the dough, adding 3 tablespoons of water and a pinch of salt. Knead well until soft and elastic. Set aside, covered with a damp piece of paper towel.

For the filling, pour boiling water over the peas and leave for five minutes, then drain and squeeze out excess water. Put the peas into a bowl. Heat the ghee in a small pan and add the mustard seeds. Once they have popped, pour into the peas with the remaining filling ingredients; mash them with a fork, season to taste, and set aside.

Add the tomato, sugar, ginger, chili powder, peanuts, and cocum, if using, to the lentils. Then heat the ghee in a small pan; add the asafetida and whole spices and, once the popping starts to subside, stir in the ground coriander and curry leaves. Cook for another two to three seconds, then pour into the lentils. Return to a boil, cover, and simmer for 15 minutes.

Meanwhile make the dumplings. Roll the dough into a rope and cut into eight equal pieces. Take one and use a little extra flour to help you roll it out into a very thin 3-inch disk. Fill with 1 tablespoon of filling and close like a pasty, folding over and pinching the seam. Repeat with the rest.

Pour enough boiling water into the lentils so they have a thin consistency. Add most of the tamarind, taste and adjust the salt, sugar, and tamarind to taste. Add the dumplings to the curry and return to a boil, then reduce the heat and simmer gently for 10 minutes. Serve in warmed soup bowls with two dumplings each.

SERVES 4

FOR THE LENTIL CURRY

1 cup split pigeon peas (toor dal), washed
salt, to taste
½ teaspoon turmeric
1 large-ish tomato, chopped
2 tablespoons jaggery or brown sugar
½-ounce gingerroot, peeled weight, grated
¼–½ teaspoon chili powder
2 tablespoons dry roasted peanuts, coarsely crushed (optional)
8 dried cocum, soaked (optional)
2 tablespoons ghee
¼ teaspoon asafetida
4 cloves
3-inch cinnamon stick
½ teaspoon each mustard and cumin seeds
¼ teaspoon fenugreek seeds
1 teaspoon ground coriander
10 curry leaves
1 teaspoon tamarind paste, dissolved in a little hot water, or to taste

FOR THE DOUGH

½ cup chapati flour, plus more to dust
¼ teaspoon each turmeric and ajowan seeds
1 tablespoon vegetable oil

FOR THE FILLING

generous 1 cup frozen peas
1 rounded teaspoon ghee
⅓ teaspoon mustard seeds
2 tablespoons dry unsweetened coconut
⅓-ounce gingerroot, peeled weight, grated
small handful of chopped cilantro leaves

This is a North Indian classic. Normally the cubes of paneer are lightly fried before being added to the sauce—which changes their texture and flavor and crisps their sides—but adding "raw" paneer, as I do here, makes it lighter and creamier. If you are making this dish earlier in the day for supper, or even a day before, then fry the paneer, as it keeps its shape better. Serve with naan or roti.

Paneer and pea curry

Heat the oil in a large nonstick pan, add the whole spices, and cook for 20 seconds. Add the onions and sauté gently until they are a deep golden brown. Add the garlic and cook for one or two minutes, or until the garlic smells cooked.

Meanwhile, blend together the tomatoes and ginger with a good splash of water until smooth. Add to the pot with the ground spices and salt. Bring to a boil, then reduce the heat to a simmer and cook down until it is a thick paste, stirring every so often in the beginning and then more as the paste thickens. Taste; it should seem harmonious with no raw elements to it.

Add the peas and tomato paste and cook for a minute or two, then pour in generous 2 cups of water and bring to a boil. Add the paneer, return to a boil, then reduce the heat and simmer for five to six minutes. Stir in the cilantro leaves and cream. Taste and adjust the seasoning, adding the sugar if it seems acidic, as well as a little extra boiling water if the curry looks too thick, then serve.

SERVES 4 TO 6

5 tablespoons vegetable oil (or half oil and half ghee, or unsalted butter, for more flavor)
4 dried or 2 fresh bay leaves
4 black cardamom pods
10 black peppercorns
2 small onions, minced
3 large garlic cloves, peeled and minced
4 large tomatoes, quartered
¾ ounce gingerroot, peeled weight
2 teaspoons ground coriander
½ teaspoon chili powder
½ teaspoon turmeric
1 teaspoon garam masala
salt, to taste
1¾ cups frozen peas
1½ tablespoons tomato paste (or more if your tomatoes aren't great)
11 ounces paneer (preferably homemade, see page 9), in ¾-inch cubes
good handful of chopped cilantro leaves
3–4 tablespoons heavy cream
pinch of superfine sugar (optional)

This dish, khao sway, came to India during the Second World War and has grown in popularity over the years. Once a simple recipe, it is now a dinner party favorite. I have added a few vegetables and some eggs, but you can vary the accompaniments to your own taste. The curry is normally served with cilantro, chiles, fried garlic, and lemons on the side, so guests add what they like. To shred the potato for the potato straws, I use the slicer part of my box grater, then finely slice the paper-thin circles into long, fine julienne; it works beautifully.

Burmese-style egg, vegetable, and noodle coconut curry

Heat the oil for the curry in a large nonstick pan. Add the fenugreek and fry until browned, then the onion. Cook over high heat until caramelized at the edges. Meanwhile, blend the tomato, ginger, and garlic with water until smooth. Add the gram flour to the onion and sauté over medium heat for one minute, scraping the pan often.

Add the tomato mixture, all the spices, and salt. Give it a good stir and cook until it thickens considerably, 12 to 15 minutes over medium-low heat, stirring often. Remove and set aside the dried chiles, add a splash of water, and blend until smooth. Pour back into the rinsed-out pan and return the chiles. Add the coconut milk and ⅔ cup of water and simmer for five minutes. Now add the coconut cream, lemon juice, and sugar. The sauce should be creamy but not too thick.

Toss the potato straws in the salt in a bowl. Gently heat 1¼ inches of oil in a pan (the wider the pan the more you can do at once). When the oil is medium-hot, squeeze out as much water as you can from the potatoes and add one or two large handfuls to the oil. Do not overcrowd the pan. Fry for five to six minutes, breaking up tangled straws, until lightly golden and crispy. Remove with a slotted spoon and drain on paper towels. Repeat to cook all the straws.

Meanwhile, boil the eggs for eight minutes. Heat 1 tablespoon of the vegetable oil in a large nonstick skillet, add the okra, season, and stir for a few minutes, then cover and cook until soft (three to four minutes). Remove. Heat another 1 tablespoon of oil in the pan and add the mushrooms, season, and fry until golden and crisp on the edges.

Cook the noodles according to the package directions and mound in the center of deep plates. Pour the sauce over and arrange the eggs, okra, and mushrooms around. Sprinkle with chopped cilantro, peanuts, and potato straws. Serve with lemon wedges and sliced chiles.

SERVES 4

FOR THE COCONUT CURRY
4–5 tablespoons vegetable oil
¼ teaspoon fenugreek seeds
1 large onion, sliced
1 large-ish tomato, quartered
¾ ounce gingerroot, peeled weight
5 garlic cloves, peeled
1 rounded tablespoon gram (chickpea) flour
2–3 dried red chiles
½ teaspoon turmeric
1 tablespoon ground coriander
1½ teaspoons ground cumin
1½ teaspoons garam masala, or to taste
salt, to taste
1¾ cups coconut milk
2 ounces coconut cream
2–3 teaspoons lemon juice, or to taste
good pinch of superfine sugar (optional)

FOR THE POTATO STRAWS (SALLI)
1 potato, shredded (see recipe introduction)
⅓ teaspoon salt
vegetable oil, to deep-fry

FOR THE REST
4–6 eggs
2 tablespoons vegetable oil
5 ounces okra, or 1 eggplant, sliced
8–12 large oyster mushrooms
8 ounces egg noodles (I like wide, flat ones)
handful of chopped cilantro leaves
4 tablespoons salted and roasted peanuts
lemon wedges, to serve
1–2 large red chiles, sliced, to serve

Black-eyed peas are absolutely delicious, delicate but with a distinctive flavor that I prefer to all other beans. They have been part of the Indian diet for thousands of years but I have never seen them on a restaurant menu, which is a pity as they make a lovely, light curry. This recipe is inspired by the West Coast of India. If you don't love coconut, you can make this without (add water instead, leave out the tamarind, and keep the curry quite thick). Serve with Indian bread or a rice pilaf, or plain boiled rice.

Black-eyed pea and coconut curry

Drain the soaked beans, tip into a large pan, and add fresh water to come 2 inches above the level of the beans. Bring to a boil, cover, and cook until just soft, around 45 minutes. Salt the beans lightly about 30 minutes into cooking. Remove from the heat and drain, setting aside generous 1–1¼ cups of the cooking water.

Heat the oil in a nonstick pan. Add the mustard seeds and, once they pop, add the curry leaves and cook for another few seconds. Add the onion and green chiles and cook until the onion is golden brown on the edges.

Meanwhile, blend together the garlic, ginger, and tomato until smooth. Add to the cooked onions with the ground cumin and coriander, chili powder, and a splash of water, and season. Cook over medium-high heat until completely reduced, stirring occasionally to start with, then more as the moisture dries up. Once the masala has released oil back into the pan and tastes harmonious, add the cooked dried beans (or canned beans, if using, and the reserved cooking liquid, or generous 1–1¼ cups of water if using canned beans. Bring to a boil and cook until all the moisture in the pot has evaporated, stirring occasionally.

Add the coconut milk and enough water to make a creamy curry (around 1 cup), return to a boil, and simmer for five minutes for the whole thing to come together. Stir in the tamarind paste and garam masala, adjust the seasoning, and serve sprinkled with the cilantro.

SERVES 4 TO 5

generous 1 cup dried black-eyed peas, washed well and soaked overnight (or 2 x 14-ounce cans, drained and rinsed well)
salt, to taste
3 tablespoons vegetable oil
1 teaspoon mustard seeds
10 curry leaves
1 small-ish onion, minced
2 green chiles, whole but pierced with the tip of a knife
3 fat garlic cloves, peeled
¾ ounce gingerroot, peeled weight
1 large-ish tomato, quartered
1 teaspoon ground cumin
1 teaspoon ground coriander
⅛–¼ teaspoon chili powder, or to taste
generous 1 cup coconut milk
⅓–½ teaspoon tamarind paste, or to taste
½–¾ teaspoon garam masala, or to taste
handful of chopped cilantro leaves

Forgot to soak overnight?

Bring the beans and enough water to cover to a boil, then boil for one minute. Remove from the heat, cover tightly, and let stand for one hour. Drain well and cook as above.

A vegetarian Indian take on the British classic pie. I cook Quorn grounds quite often, as my daughter and I love it. Sometimes it's eaten with Indian breads, other times with buttered bread, and here it is topped with creamy, cheesy mashed potatoes to make a substantial, delicious one-pot meal. You can also omit the Quorn and make the dish with some Puy lentils or a mixture of lentils and beans, if you prefer. Whichever way you make this, it is delicious and very satisfying. I serve greens on the side.

Luscious spiced cottage pie

Heat the vegetable oil and add the onion, cardamom pods, and bay leaves. Cook until the onion is starting to color at the edges. Preheat the oven to 400°F.

Using a stick blender, blend the chunk of ginger and the garlic with a little water until smooth. Separately blend the tomatoes until smooth. Add the ginger and garlic paste to the onion and cook gently. Once the garlic has started to color, add the tomatoes, tomato paste, and the remaining spices and seasoning. Cook over medium-high heat, stirring occasionally, until the masala has thickened, looks like a tomato paste, and releases oil back into the pan. Taste, it should be harmonious with no sharp notes. Add the grounds and stir-fry for three to four minutes. Now pour in 1¾ cups of water, bring to a boil, then reduce the heat and simmer until most of the liquid has been absorbed. Add the peas after three minutes. Taste and adjust the seasoning, making sure you have added a good pinch of black pepper, and add lemon juice if it needs it. Stir in the chopped cilantro and turn off the heat.

Meanwhile, place the potatoes in a pan of cold water, bring to a boil, and cook until just tender to the point of a knife. Drain well and let them dry off in the pan for a minute. Using a potato ricer or masher, mash well, add the butter, milk, and cheese, and mash and stir until amalgamated; I like mine a little lumpy. Season to taste, adding lots of black pepper.

Spoon the grounds evenly into an ovenproof, table-ready dish. Pipe or spoon on the mashed potato to cover, decorate as you like (not at all, or with the tines of a fork). If you would like a golden finish, dot the surface all over with small cubes of butter. Place in the middle of the oven and bake for 30 minutes, or until golden. Serve hot.

SERVES 4 GENEROUSLY

FOR THE FILLING
3 tablespoons vegetable oil
1 onion, minced
3 black cardamom pods
2 bay leaves
¾ ounce gingerroot, peeled weight,
    ⅓ ounce of it sliced into fine julienne
3 garlic cloves, peeled
2 tomatoes, quartered
1 tablespoon tomato paste, or to taste
2 teaspoons ground coriander
¼–½ teaspoon chili powder, or to taste
1 teaspoon garam masala
1 teaspoon ground cumin
salt, to taste
freshly ground black pepper, to taste
12 ounces Quorn (or other vegetarian
    grounds)
2 small handfuls of frozen peas
lemon juice, to taste
large handful of chopped cilantro leaves

FOR THE TOPPING
1¼ pounds mealy potatoes, peeled and cut in
    large pieces
¼ cup (½ stick) unsalted butter, plus more
    to cook (optional)
generous ¼–generous ⅓ cup whole milk
2–2¼ ounces sharp cheddar cheese

One of our staple Sunday lunches, this is a Punjabi stalwart, loved by meat-eaters and vegetarians alike. It seems to be a dish that Indians across the subcontinent appreciate, regardless of their own regional cuisine, and one I get plenty of requests for online. So here it is. It might not look great on paper, but it is wonderful on the plate. I really prefer dried kidney beans here, as they have more flavor and a better texture. This does mean overnight soaking and a long cook in the morning, but aside from some forethought it's no harder than using canned, and is more rewarding. (When I tested the recipe with canned beans, the sauce needed some help, see below.) Serve with plain basmati rice.

Sunday lunch kidney bean curry

Drain the soaked beans and tip them into a large pan. Cover with fresh water and bring to a boil. Boil hard for 10 minutes, then reduce the heat to a lively simmer and cook for 1½ to 1¾ hours. After they have been cooking for 1¼ hours, blend the onion with a little water until smooth. Separately blend the ginger and garlic in the same way.

Heat the oil in a large nonstick skillet, add the onion paste, and cook until really well browned (it should look like chocolate), stirring often as it starts to brown. Add the ginger and garlic paste and cook until you can smell the garlic is cooked, around one minute after the water has dried up. Meanwhile, blend the tomatoes with a stick blender until smooth and add them to the pan with the spices and seasoning. Cook this on medium-low heat until it is completely cooked through and is very thick, resembling tomato paste, around 25 minutes.

Drain the cooked kidney beans and set aside the cooking liquor. Add the beans to the tomato sauce and stir for one minute, then pour in scant 2 cups of the bean cooking liquor, bring to a boil, reduce the heat, and simmer for five minutes. Throw in the chopped cilantro, taste, adjust the seasoning, and serve.

SERVES 3 TO 4

generous 1 cup dried kidney beans, washed well and soaked overnight (if you have to use canned beans, see below)
1 small onion, roughly chopped
½-ounce gingerroot, peeled weight, roughly chopped
2 fat garlic cloves, peeled
4 tablespoons vegetable oil
2 large-ish tomatoes, quartered
1½ teaspoons ground coriander
1 rounded teaspoon ground cumin
¾ teaspoon garam masala
¼–½ teaspoon chili powder, to taste
salt, to taste
large handful of chopped cilantro leaves

Cooking canned?

Use 2 x 14-ounce cans, drained and rinsed. You need to help out the flavorings, so add a bit more of everything else. Try 1 medium onion, 4 garlic cloves, ¾ ounce gingerroot, and a little more ground cumin and coriander and garam masala. The method is the same. This version will have a slightly thicker sauce.

A great Goan classic sauce which has a rich tomato flavor rounded off with delicately balanced, spicy, salty, sour, and slightly sweet tastes. It works really well with eggs. This dish is very addictive and is one I crave often ... eating scrambled or fried eggs no longer has the same appeal. If you are a duck egg fan, this is great with the richer yolks. I like to serve this with rotis or parathas.

Goan egg balchao

Using a stick blender, blend the ginger and garlic with a little water until smooth. Separately blend the tomatoes until smooth. Grind the whole spices and chiles to a powder using a mortar and pestle or a spice grinder.

Heat the oil in a nonstick pan. Add the onions and cook over medium-high heat until well browned on the edges, stirring often. Add the ginger and garlic paste and cook over medium heat, stirring once the water has evaporated, until the garlic has colored lightly and the paste has released its oil. Add the tomatoes to the cooked masala with the ground spices, seasoning, and sugar and cook over high heat until it has completely reduced.

Meanwhile, put the eggs onto boil for seven to eight minutes. Take out of the hot water and plunge into cold water to stop the cooking. Once the sauce has reduced, keeping the heat at medium-high, "brown" the paste until it has darkened considerably, stirring very often. This will really add a lot of depth of flavor.

Once the paste is cooked through, add the vinegar and a good splash of water and simmer until you have a thick sauce. Meanwhile, peel your eggs and halve lengthwise. Taste the sauce and adjust the salt, sugar, and vinegar, add the eggs, and simmer for a few minutes. The sauce should cling to the eggs. Serve hot.

SERVES 4

1 ounce gingerroot, peeled weight
10 garlic cloves, peeled
4 large vine tomatoes, quartered
2 teaspoons cumin seeds
3 teaspoons mustard seeds
8 cloves
24 black peppercorns
3–5 dried Kashmiri red chiles, whole
6 tablespoons vegetable oil
2 onions, chopped
salt, to taste
$2^2/_3$ teaspoons superfine sugar, or to taste
8 large eggs
4 tablespoons white wine vinegar, or to taste

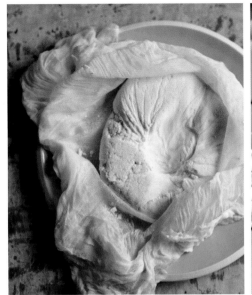

This is definitely a special occasion dish, as it is elegant as well as delicious, and worth the effort if you have people coming around. Normally, I stuff the koftas with a spiced mushroom mixture but, as I was writing the recipe, it seemed one step too far and fiddly ... so I decided to deconstruct the dish, adding lovely shiitake mushrooms separately, which actually works better. If you want, you can choose to stuff the balls simply with a raisin and a pistachio each. If your paneer is store bought, place it in just-boiled water while you work on the sauce, to improve the texture and flavor.

Paneer koftas and shiitake mushroom curry

Soak the cashews in water for 15 minutes, then drain. Blend to a smooth paste with 1–2 tablespoons of water, then set aside. Heat the oil for the sauce in a large nonstick pan. Add the black cardamom and onions and cook until well browned. Add the ginger and garlic and cook until lightly coloring. Add the tomatoes, tomato paste, remaining spices, and seasoning; cook over medium heat, stirring, until the water evaporates and the paste releases oil, around 15 minutes. Cook the paste for a few minutes over moderate-high heat, stirring constantly, to get a better depth of flavor. Add a splash of water, then blend to a paste. Add enough water to reach the consistency of light cream, bring to a boil, cover, and simmer for six to seven minutes.

While the curry is cooking, make the koftas. Break up and crumble the paneer until it is fine then, with the heel of your hand, knead until it is even finer (when you squeeze a bit together, it should hold). The more you work it, the smoother it becomes. Add ½ teaspoon of salt and the cilantro leaves and form into large marble-sized balls.

Add enough oil to come 2 inches up the sides of a small pan and heat to 350°F. Test the oil by dropping in a small amount of the mixture; it should sizzle immediately but not color straightaway. Add a batch of koftas so that the pan is not overcrowded, then cook, turning halfway, until deep golden. Remove with a slotted spoon and drain on paper towels. Repeat with the remaining koftas. Remove most of the remaining oil from the pan, leaving around 1–2 tablespoons, then add the mushrooms, season lightly, and sauté for four to five minutes.

Once the curry is done, add the cashew paste and the cream and bring to a gentle simmer; the consistency should be of a light cream. Add the koftas and mushrooms, return to a boil, then reduce the heat, cover, and simmer for five minutes. Taste and adjust the seasoning. Sprinkle over the dried fenugreek and add a swirl of cream and a sprinkling of chopped cilantro.

SERVES 5 TO 6

FOR THE SAUCE
⅓ cup cashews
8 tablespoons vegetable oil
3 black cardamom pods
2 large onions, sliced
1 ounce gingerroot, peeled weight, grated
4 fat garlic cloves, peeled and grated
4 large tomatoes, quartered
2 tablespoons tomato paste
½–¾ teaspoon chili powder
1 rounded tablespoon ground coriander
1¾ teaspoons ground cumin
⅓ teaspoon turmeric
2 teaspoons garam masala
salt, to taste
5–6 tablespoons heavy cream, plus more to serve
1 rounded teaspoon dried fenugreek leaves

FOR THE KOFTAS AND MUSHROOMS
12 ounces paneer (preferably homemade, see page 9)
small handful of chopped cilantro leaves, plus more to serve
vegetable oil, to deep-fry
12 shiitake mushrooms, stalks discarded, thickly sliced, or halved if small

This is a really lovely black pepper and fennel-flecked sauce, reminiscent of the spicy food of South India, where black pepper is the king of spices. I have used it here as a base for cooking dried soy chunks. This is one ingredient that you either love or don't! It is a derivate of the soybean and is full of protein. I love soy in its many guises and enjoy the slightly chewy texture of these chunks but, if you don't, you can replace it with 9 ounces of paneer or a couple of 14-ounce cans of chickpeas. Serve with roti, paratha, or even buttered toast.

Southern black pepper curry

Heat the oil in a nonstick pan, then add the fennel seeds and half the black pepper, and cook until the fennel is starting to color. Add the curry leaves and cook for another few seconds. Add the onion and sauté until golden brown. Meanwhile, using a stick blender, blend the tomatoes until smooth.

Add the ginger and garlic to the cooked onion and gently sauté until the garlic smells cooked, around one minute. Pour in the tomatoes along with the ground spices, salt, and tomato paste. Cook this down until it releases oil back into the pan; it will probably be quite thick.

Squeeze the water out of the soaking soy, add to the pan, and cook for a minute or two. Add enough water to nearly cover the chunks. Bring to a boil and simmer until the chunks are soft but still chewy, around four to five minutes. By now the sauce should have reduced.

Add the remaining black pepper, taste, adjust the seasoning, and serve. The sauce should cling to the soy chunks.

SERVES 4

5 tablespoons vegetable oil
1 teaspoon fennel seeds
2 teaspoons freshly crushed black pepper, or to taste
10 fresh curry leaves
1 onion, minced
2 large tomatoes, quartered
1-ounce gingerroot, peeled weight, grated
5 large garlic cloves, peeled and grated
2 teaspoons ground coriander
1½ teaspoons ground cumin
salt, to taste
1 tablespoon tomato paste
3½ ounces soy chunks (or see recipe introduction), soaked in boiling water for 15 minutes

GORGEOUS
GRAINS

The perfect combination of drama, show, and pomp. This dish requires a little effort, but all it needs to go with it is a raita and perhaps a salad on the side. I like to use a few different types of mushroom for varying textures and flavors and, if the budget allows, to add a few wild mushrooms. If not, stick to shiitake, oyster, and large cremini mushrooms. The pastry is lovely on top but you can leave it off and finish the dish with the saffron and some roasted cashews instead. The cream and tomato paste are there to balance the flavors of the sauce, so add to taste, and season the sauce well.

Wild mushroom biryani

Start with the mushrooms. Blend together the tomatoes and yogurt until smooth. Heat the oil in a large nonstick pan. Add the onions and cook until golden on the edges. Add the ginger and garlic and cook gently until the smell of raw garlic has disappeared, around a minute or so. Add the blended tomatoes, all the spices, and the salt and give the pan a stir. Cook this mixture down until it becomes a thick paste and releases oil back into the pan, then continue cooking for another couple of minutes to darken.

Stir in the mushrooms and cook for four to five minutes, or until they release their water (cover the pan after two minutes, but keep giving it a stir). Add ⅔ cup of water and bring to a boil, then simmer for seven to eight minutes or until the whole thing comes together. Add the tomato paste and the cream. Taste and adjust the seasoning, adding more cream or tomato paste to balance the sourness in the tomatoes and yogurt. The sauce should be like thick cream. Take off the heat.

For the rice, heat the oil in a large pan. Add the whole spices and cook for 30 seconds. Add the drained rice and stir well. Add 4 cups of boiling water and season generously to taste. Bring to a boil, then cover and cook on really low heat until the rice is just done, around seven to nine minutes (check after seven). Take off the heat.

Preheat the oven to 425°F. Find a suitable dish that is both ovenproof and table ready. Layer half the rice in the dish, then spoon all the mushrooms and sauce evenly over it. Sprinkle over the herbs and finish with the remaining rice. Drizzle over the saffron milky cream. Roll out the pastry on a floured counter to fit the dish, sprinkling with the fenugreek leaves, if using, and a little sea salt, pressing them in so they stay in place. Lift the pastry over the dish, sealing the edges and trimming away excess. Brush with egg, if using. Bake for 30 minutes, or until the pastry is golden and cooked all the way through, then serve.

SERVES 7 TO 8

FOR THE MUSHROOMS

4 large-ish tomatoes, quartered
generous ¾ cup yogurt
5 tablespoons vegetable oil
2 onions, minced
1 ounce gingerroot, peeled weight, grated
6 large garlic cloves, peeled and grated
1 teaspoon chili powder
1½ teaspoons ground cumin
¾ teaspoon turmeric
2 teaspoons garam masala
salt, to taste
1¾ pounds mixed mushrooms, cleaned and
    sliced or torn into large pieces
1 rounded tablespoon tomato paste, to taste
¼ cup heavy cream, or to taste

FOR THE RICE

5 tablespoons vegetable oil
2 black cardamom pods
5 each of cloves and green cardamom pods
4-inch cinnamon stick
10 black peppercorns
3¼ cups basmati rice, well washed, then
    soaked for 20 minutes
small handful of shredded mint leaves
small handful of chopped cilantro leaves
good pinch of saffron strands, soaked in
    2 tablespoons hot milk and 1 tablespoon
    heavy cream for 30 minutes
9 ounces puff pastry
all-purpose flour, to dust
½ teaspoon dried fenugreek leaves (optional)
sea salt, to taste
1 egg, beaten (optional)

Beaten rice—poha or powa—is cooked rice that has been flattened into a flake. It is a really interesting ingredient as it is very light and fluffy and has a lovely texture, and you only have to steam it to heat through. This dish is very popular in many parts of India and normally eaten for breakfast. I love it as a light, quick lunch, with a few vegetables. It really is worth seeking out from Indian stores. Don't confuse it with the flaked rice you can find in supermarkets, as that is raw, so cooks differently. This dish would be eaten at breakfast in India, but I mainly make it for a light lunch.

Beaten rice pilaf with peas, potatoes, and carrots

Heat the oil in a nonstick pan. Add the lentils and cook gently until just coloring. Add the mustard seeds and curry leaves and, once the popping dies down, the onion, and green chiles, and cook until the onion is just soft. Add the ginger and cook for another minute.

Add the vegetables, salt, turmeric, and a small splash of water; give the pan a good stir, bring to a boil, cover, and cook for six to seven minutes or until the vegetables are cooked through, checking halfway and giving them a stir.

Quickly wash the rice in some water and add to the pan with another 2 tablespoons of water. Cover and steam for three to four minutes, then stir in the lemon juice and check if the flakes are soft. Take off the heat, cover, and leave for another minute. Taste, adjust the seasoning, and serve.

SERVES 2, CAN BE DOUBLED

2 tablespoons vegetable oil
2 teaspoons Bengal gram (chana dal), well washed
1 teaspoon brown mustard seeds
8–10 curry leaves
½ onion, minced
1–2 green chiles, whole but pierced with the tip of a knife
¼ ounce gingerroot, peeled weight, minced
scant ½ cup peas
2 ounces potatoes, cut into 1-inch pieces
2 ounces cauliflower, cut into 1-inch florets
1¼ ounces carrots, cut into ½-inch dice
salt, to taste
½ teaspoon turmeric
5 ounces beaten rice (see recipe introduction)
2½–3½ teaspoons lemon juice, or to taste

Quinoa needs little introduction these days, it is such a healthy grain that it pops up everywhere. Vegetarians should definitely include it in their diet, as it is high in good-quality protein. This pilaf is a particularly lovely way to cook and eat quinoa. If you don't have ruby chard, use any other leaf in season, from spinach to savoy cabbage. The cannellini beans add a lovely creaminess, but feel free to substitute any other bean. I find I eat this pilaf as it is and need little else with it, but you can also eat it with a chutney or a raita.

Cannellini bean, ruby chard, and quinoa pilaf

Place the quinoa in a pan of water, bring to a boil, reduce the heat, and simmer until just done, 16 to 18 minutes for mine (see the package directions, but check as it cooks). It will look like it has burst a little. Drain well, then return to the hot pan, off the heat.

Wash, then shred or cut the ruby chard as you prefer. I like to use mostly leaf with just a little stalk, shredded, for color and texture.

Meanwhile, heat the oil in a nonstick pan. Add the cumin and mustard seeds and the dried chile and cook until the mustard stops popping and the cumin has colored. Add the onion and cook until soft and coloring at the edges. Stir in the garlic, reduce the heat, and cook for a minute. Add the chard, season with salt, and give the pot a good stir, then cover and cook over medium heat until the chard is soft, anywhere from four to six minutes, stirring occasionally.

Add the beans, some black pepper, and the lemon juice and cook until the beans are heated through. Add the drained quinoa and fold through with a fork. Taste, adjust the seasoning and lemon juice, then serve.

SERVES 2, CAN BE DOUBLED

scant 1 cup quinoa
2 handfuls of ruby chard
3 tablespoons vegetable oil
$2/3$ teaspoon cumin seeds
¾ teaspoon mustard seeds
1 dried red chile
1 red onion, minced
3 large garlic cloves, peeled and grated
salt, to taste
14-ounce can cannellini beans, drained and rinsed
freshly ground black pepper
2–2½ teaspoons lemon juice, or to taste

Most recipes on this side of the world that use bulgur wheat are salads, but Indians, particularly the Gujarati people, use it regularly in pilaf. This is a lovely, delicate dish that my mother-in-law first cooked for me after I had my first child: nourishing for a slightly depleted new mom, but light on the system. I so loved the simple flavors and nuttiness of the bulgur that it has remained in my diet; my daughter is now six. Vary the vegetables, using what you have. I eat it with yogurt and a good turn of black pepper. If you won't be eating it with yogurt, add a little lemon juice at the end. I usually cook this just for my little family. You can double the recipe but, if you do, only use 6 cloves and 15 peppercorns.

Vegetable and lentil bulgur

Heat the ghee in a nonstick skillet. Add the whole spices and cook until the cumin is aromatic. Add the onion and sauté until soft. Add the ginger and garlic and cook gently for one minute, or until the garlic smells cooked and has turned lightly golden.

Add the vegetables, lentils, ground spices, salt, and a splash of water. Bring to a boil, stir well, cover, and simmer until the vegetables are almost cooked, around five minutes. Uncover the pan to drive off any excess water.

Add the bulgur wheat and stir well. Mix in 1¼ cups of boiling water, cover, and cook over low heat for 13 to 15 minutes. Check a grain: it should be cooked, if not place back on the heat to steam a little more. Take off the heat but let steam, covered, for another five minutes or so. Taste, adjust the seasoning, and serve.

SERVES 2 TO 3

1½ tablespoons ghee, or a mixture of
  unsalted butter and vegetable oil
2-inch cinnamon stick
4 cloves
1 teaspoon cumin seeds
12 black peppercorns
1 small-ish onion, chopped
scant ½ ounce gingerroot, peeled weight,
  grated
2 garlic cloves, peeled and grated
¼ cup yellow lentils (mung dal), washed well
1 teaspoon ground coriander
¾ teaspoon ground cumin
¾ teaspoon garam masala
salt, to taste
scant 1 cup bulgur wheat

VEGETABLES I HAVE USED HERE:
6–7 green beans, chopped into ¾-inch
  lengths (or a handful of peas)
2 ounces cauliflower, cut into 1-inch florets
2 ounces broccoli, cut into 1-inch florets
⅓ small red bell pepper, cut into ⅝-inch cubes

This is a Tamil dish, made with leftover rice, yogurt, and milk. It is delicate in flavor and consistency and perfect for the warmer months, as it is quite refreshing and filling but not heavy. It is lovely as it is, or as a creamy side dish with a vegetable or lentil recipe, or spoon over a little of the Southern Tomato Chutney or Coastal Coconut Chutney (see below and page 19).

Creamy yogurt rice

Bring the rice to a boil in a large pot of water. Simmer for eight or nine minutes, or until soft. Drain, then return the pan to low heat for two minutes to drive off the moisture. Cover and leave off the heat.

Heat the oil in a small pan. Add the mustard and cumin seeds. Once the popping slows down, add the chile and curry leaves, and follow a few seconds later with both types of lentil. Once the larger ones starts to color, add the ginger and cook for another minute. Pour the whole thing into the pot of rice with the milk, yogurt, and salt.

Stir well over low heat. Taste and adjust the seasoning and yogurt, depending upon how sour it is and how loose you want the consistency. It should be creamy and oatmeal-like. Serve warm.

SERVES 4 TO 6

scant 1 cup basmati rice, well washed in several changes of water
2 tablespoons vegetable oil or ghee
1 teaspoon mustard seeds
¾ teaspoon cumin seeds
1 dried red chile, broken in half
8–10 fresh curry leaves
1 teaspoon Bengal gram (chana dal), well washed
1 teaspoon black gram (urad dal), well washed
¼ ounce gingerroot, peeled weight, minced
generous 1 cup whole milk
generous 1–1½ cups yogurt, depending on sourness
salt, to taste

Southern tomato chutney
MAKES SCANT ⅓ CUP

A lovely spicy, tangy chutney full of the flavors of South India.
   Heat 1 tablespoon of vegetable oil in a small nonstick pan over medium heat. Add ½ small onion, sliced, and cook until softening. Add ⅛ ounce of peeled gingerroot and 2 fat, peeled garlic cloves and fry over gentle heat for one minute. Add 3 small ripe tomatoes, chopped, and salt, cover, and cook for five minutes. Blend until smooth, then return to the pan. Heat ¼ tablespoon more oil in a separate pan. Add 1 teaspoon of washed Bengal gram (chana dal) and cook until starting to color. Add 2 dried chiles, ½ teaspoon each of mustard and cumin seeds, and a pinch of fenugreek seeds and cook over gentle heat for 20 seconds, or until the seeds darken. Add 8 curry leaves, give them five seconds, then pour the contents of the pan into the chutney. Return the chutney to the heat and add ¼ teaspoon of tamarind paste, or to taste. Adjust the seasoning and serve.

A biryani is a really special dish from the Moghuls, who made India their home many centuries ago. Originally made with all the ingredients they loved—lamb, rice, saffron, nuts, and butter—it now can be made with any ingredient. This version consists of layers of spice-flecked rice hiding a layer of vegetables cooked in a rich sauce. I have departed from tradition and topped it with a layer of delicious fried potatoes and crispy onions. It is a multistage dish, but then it is for a special occasion and needs little more than yogurt on the side. (Try it with yogurt into which you have stirred some chopped cilantro leaves, shredded mint leaves, and seasoning.)

Elegant vegetable biryani

Bring the drained rice and whole spices to a boil in salted water to cover by 1¼–1½ inches. Simmer for four to six minutes, until just done. Drain the water, return the rice to the heat, allow excess moisture to evaporate for 10 seconds, then set aside. Heat the milk and saffron for assembling the dish together, then set aside.

For the vegetables, heat the oil in a large nonstick pan. Add the onion and cook until lightly golden. Add the ginger and garlic and continue cooking until the garlic has turned light golden. Meanwhile, using a stick blender, blend the tomatoes until smooth. Add the spices and tomatoes to the cooked onion, season, then cook down until the tomatoes are getting thick. Add the carrot, cover, and cook for five minutes. Stir in the cauliflower, eggplants, mushrooms, and yogurt. Bring to a boil, stirring often, then cover and simmer until the vegetables are cooked through, around 10 minutes, adding the peas after five minutes. Add the cream, taste, and adjust the seasoning.

Choose a large ovenproof dish that has a tight-fitting lid and is table worthy. Butter the bottom liberally. Spread in half the rice, breaking up any clumps. Season lightly and drizzle over some saffron milk. Spoon over the vegetables, then the remaining rice. Drizzle over the remaining saffron milk, season, then evenly dot cubes of butter on top. Cover.

About 40 minutes before dinner, place the dish in a very large skillet half-filled with water, to make sure nothing burns. Warm it through for 40 to 45 minutes, or until you can see the rice steaming inside. (Or cook in an oven preheated to 325°F for 30 to 40 minutes, or until heated through.)

Meanwhile, deep-fry the sliced onion until deep golden brown. Remove with a slotted spoon and drain on paper towels. Add the potatoes to the oil and fry until golden and cooked; place on paper towels and sprinkle with salt and chaat masala. Keep these warm. Just before serving, top the biryani with the potatoes and crisp onions.

SERVES 5 TO 6

FOR THE RICE
2¼ cups basmati rice, washed well, then soaked for 20 to 30 minutes
6 cloves
6 green cardamom pods
3 black cardamom pods
2 x 3-inch cinnamon sticks
2 bay leaves

TO ASSEMBLE
4 tablespoons whole milk
large pinch of saffron strands
½–1½ tablespoons unsalted butter
vegetable oil, to deep-fry
1 large onion, sliced
2 potatoes, peeled and thinly sliced
chaat masala (see page 58)

FOR THE VEGETABLES
5 tablespoons vegetable oil
1 large onion, minced
1¼ ounces gingerroot, peeled weight, grated
5 fat garlic cloves, peeled and grated
3 tomatoes, quartered
3 teaspoons ground coriander
1½ teaspoons ground cumin
2 rounded teaspoons garam masala
½–1 teaspoon chili power, to taste
1 small carrot, peeled and in ½-inch slies
11 ounces cauliflower, in 1-inch florets
4 small Japanese eggplants, in 1-inch slices
5 large cremini mushrooms, thickly sliced
scant ⅔ cup yogurt
2 handfuls of peas
3 tablespoons heavy cream

This is a really delicious, South Indian-inspired rice dish. The style is typical of the region, with its spicy robust flavors. It is normally made with a coarser, whiter rice of that region, but I use basmati as it is the easiest to find and works well. If you have a hardier rice, now is a good time to use it! This is not supposed to be a fluffy rice dish, in fact it is normally slightly wet and sloppy, but I have made it somewhere in between. It needs little more than some yogurt on the side.

Spiced eggplant and tamarind rice

Wash the rice well in several changes of water and let soak in enough water to cover well.

Heat the oil in a large pan. Add the mustard seeds and, once the popping dies down, add the curry leaves and the onion; cook until the onion starts to color on the edges. Add the garlic and cook over gentle heat for 40 seconds or until the garlic starts to color. Add the tomato, salt, turmeric, and chili powder with a splash of water and cook over medium-high heat, stirring often, for four to five minutes.

Drain the rice, then add it and the eggplants to the pan and give them a good stir in the spices. Add 1⅔ cups of water, bring to a boil, then cover and cook over really low heat until the rice has cooked through, around eight to 10 minutes.

As the rice cooks, roast your spices. Heat a skillet (I use a small cast-iron pancake pan), add the Bengal gram, and cook, stirring often, until they turn a lovely golden brown; pour into a spice grinder or mortar. Add the smaller lentils to the pan and repeat until these have gently browned; add to the spice grinder. Add the remaining spices to the pan and roast, shaking, until the cumin and coriander have darkened and are aromatic. Add to the lentils and grind to a powder.

Once the rice has cooked, uncover and add the spice powder and tamarind. Stir well with a fork, adjusting the seasoning as you do. Then cover and let steam, off the heat, for a few minutes. Stir in the chopped cilantro and sprinkle over the coconut, if using.

SERVES 4

FOR THE RICE
1¾ cups basmati rice
6 tablespoons vegetable oil
1 teaspoon mustard seeds
10–12 fresh curry leaves
1 large-ish onion, sliced
2 fat garlic cloves, peeled and chopped
1 large tomato, chopped
salt, to taste
½ teaspoon turmeric
½–1 teaspoon chili powder
36 long Japanese eggplants, cut into
    2–3 pieces depending on length
2 teaspoons tamarind paste, dissolved in
    4 tablespoons boiling water
2 handfuls of chopped cilantro leaves
2 handfuls of fresh grated coconut (optional)

FOR THE SPICE BLEND
2 tablespoons Bengal gram (chana dal),
    well washed
1 tablespoon black gram (urad dal),
    well washed
6 green cardamom pods
6 cloves
2¾-inch cinnamon stick
3 teaspoons coriander seeds
⅔ teaspoon fenugreek seeds
1½ teaspoons cumin seeds
12 black peppercorns

Rice is one of the simplest and quickest grains to cook, and good rice is addictive, yet so many people are afraid of cooking it properly. But the technique to cook great fluffy rice is actually really easy. This is how we have always made it in my family; it is foolproof. You can go on to use this simple method to create lovely pilafs.

Perfect boiled rice

Wash the rice really well in several changes of water until the water runs clear. Place in a pan and cover with at least 3 inches of water. Bring to a boil, then reduce the heat to halfway between a simmer and a boil and cook, uncovered, for seven to eight minutes. Try a grain, it should be tender; if not cook for another minute and check again.

Drain, then return the rice to the pan and the heat to dry off any moisture for one or two minutes. Turn off the heat, cover tightly, and steam for eight to 10 minutes. Uncover, fluff with a fork, and serve.

generous ⅓–scant ½ cup good-quality white basmati rice for each person

Everyone needs a pilaf recipe to pull out when you have friends to dinner. This is simple, and you can ring the changes by adding peas or carrots, or fried nuts and raisins for a sweeter version. If you are feeling generous, leave out the turmeric and substitute a good pinch of saffron. It's good with the Royal Raita (see right).

Classic yellow pilaf

Wash the rice in several changes of water until the water runs clear, then let soak as you prepare the dish. Heat the oil in a large-ish pan. Add the whole spices and fry for 30 seconds. Add the onion and fry until golden.

Add the turmeric and turn in the oil for five seconds. Add the drained rice and stir gently. Pour in 3½ cups of water, season, bring to a boil, and simmer for one minute. Cover tightly and reduce the heat to a minimum. Leave undisturbed. Check after seven minutes; there should be no water left and the rice should be cooked, or nearly so. Cook for another minute or two if necessary. Turn off the heat and leave for five to 10 minutes, then fluff with a fork and serve.

SERVES 4 TO 6

2¼ cups basmati rice
4 tablespoons vegetable oil
1¾ teaspoons cumin seeds
3 black cardamom pods
2 x 2-inch cassia barks or cinnamon sticks
6 cloves
6 green cardamom pods
1 onion, finely sliced
⅔ teaspoon turmeric
salt, to taste

This is based on a street food of Mumbai. It is made from cooked rice and vegetables stir-fried with Indian flavorings and a special spice blend on a large, flat, cast-iron pan. It becomes smoky, spicy, and tangy. I normally eat brown basmati rice at home, and the nuttiness works really well in this dish. You can add whichever leftover vegetables you have lying around. Here I have kept it simple and made it with just bell peppers and peas.

Stir-fried leftover spicy tomato and pea rice

Heat the oil in a large skillet. Add the onion and cook over high heat until browning at the edges. Add the pepper and chile and cook for another two or three minutes, or until the onion has well-browned edges. Add the garlic and cook on low heat for 40 seconds, stirring. Add the tomato, spices, and salt and cook over medium-high heat, mashing the whole thing together, for six to seven minutes.

Add a splash of water from the kettle along with the peas and cook for two or three minutes. Taste to make sure the spices are not raw or powdery and that everything tastes harmonious. Add the rice and stir-fry over high heat, adding a couple of spoons of water, until the whole thing comes together in a lovely hot mass. Taste, adjust the seasoning, and serve with lime or lemon wedges on the side.

SERVES 1, CAN BE DOUBLED

1 tablespoon vegetable oil
½ small-ish onion, sliced
½ small red or orange bell pepper, in ¾-inch cubes
1 green chile, whole but pierced with the tip of a knife
2 garlic cloves, peeled and mincedd
1 tomato, chopped
¾ teaspoon ground cumin
¼ teaspoon chili powder, or to taste
¼ teaspoon turmeric
¾ teaspoon ground coriander
½ teaspoon dried mango powder
½ teaspoon garam masala
salt, to taste
large handful of frozen peas
1–generous 1 cup cooked brown basmati rice (around ½ cup raw brown rice, boiled)
lime or lemon wedges, to serve

Royal raita
SERVES 4

Based on the flavors the Moghuls loved: rose water, fruits, and nuts. It's a great, fruity accompaniment to an Indian meal.

Cut a Pink Lady apple into ½-inch dice (leave the skin on); you'll need 4¾ ounces of diced apple. Halve 3½ ounces of white grapes, too. Put the apples and grapes in a bowl and mix in scant ¼ cup each of raisins and pistachios and 1¼ cups of yogurt. Now season with ½ teaspoon of ground cardamom, 2½–3 teaspoons of superfine sugar, and up to 1½ teaspoon of rose essence or rose water. (Be careful with the latter, adding just drops at a time before mixing and tasting, as they can vary in strength.) Serve, sprinkled with more pistachios if you like.

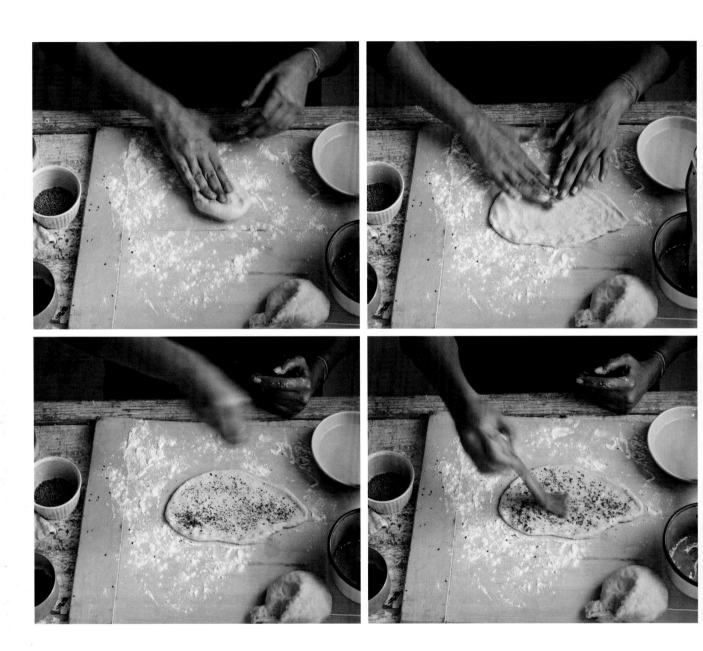

Every time I make naan, I wonder why I don't do so more often. They are so easy and my daughter always comes into the kitchen, bringing her own rolling pin with her. We get stuck in, measuring, kneading, then patiently waiting until we can finish them off; it is lots of fun and good bonding time. This broiled naan is really delicious, crispy on top and soft underneath. I love to top mine with nigella or sesame seeds, or dried mint; my six-year-old daughter stuffs hers with a mound of grated cheddar cheese (see below for her favorite recipe). Stuffing the bread is a great thing to do, and my favorite contains lovely crumbly feta, chopped mint and cilantro, minced green chiles, and onions.

Best ever broiled naan

Mix the yeast and half the sugar in 4 tablespoons of the water. Let rest for 10 minutes, or until frothy.

Stir together all the dry ingredients, including the remaining sugar. Make a well in the middle and add all the liquids except the oil. Using a fork, bring the dough together. Take it out of the bowl and knead for six to seven minutes, until soft and smooth (it will be slightly sticky at first). Oil the outside of the dough and place in a large bowl, cover with a dish towel, and leave in a warm place for at least two to three hours.

Heat the broiler (mine is in my oven) to its highest setting. Place a broiler rack or baking sheet on the upper shelf. Punch down the dough, flour a counter, and divide the dough into six. It should be very soft. Using a little extra flour, roll or pat each portion into naans that are really thin, ideally less than ½ inch thick. (I pat and roll mine into teardrop shapes.) Scatter with the topping, if using, and press lightly in, then brush with some butter.

Place on the hot baking sheet or broiler rack and broil until the surface has some lovely golden spots, about three to four minutes, then flip and broil for another two minutes or so until the other side has also cooked through. Brush the top side with a little more butter and serve.

MAKES 6 MEDIUM-LARGE NAANS

FOR THE DOUGH
¾ teaspoon dried yeast
3 teaspoons superfine sugar
generous ½–scant ⅔ cup warm water
scant 2¼ cups all-purpose flour, plus more
    to dust
scant 1 teaspoon salt
4 tablespoons melted unsalted butter, plus
    more to broil and to serve
4 tablespoons yogurt
a little vegetable oil

TOPPING OR FILLING OPTIONS
nigella, cumin, poppy, or sesame seeds,
    cilantro, mint, lightly cooked onions, chiles,
    grated cheese ... or a combination!

Mahi's stuffed broiled naan-wiches

Place a small handful of your favorite hard cheese, grated, in the middle of your rolled-out naan. Bring up the sides and pinch them together like making a bag. Pinch them until they eventually disappear back into the dough. Then flatten with your palms and roll out again. Let mom cook them.

These are the various names for the same basic, everyday whole wheat flatbreads. They are soft and puff up when cooked and, if you have a gas cooker, become a little crisp on the underside. Don't worry about not rolling a perfect circle, practice makes perfect. You can find chapati flour (atta) in most large supermarkets, but if you can't get hold of any, use equal quantities of whole wheat and all-purpose flour. These can be made in advance and reheated, wrapped in foil, in a medium oven. I never put salt in these as they are used to mop up well-seasoned sauces, but others do, so I leave it up to you.

Roti/chapati/phulka

Sift the flour and salt, if using, into a bowl and make a well in the center. Slowly drizzle in generous ¾–generous 1 cup of water and use your hand to draw the flour into the center, mixing all the time. You may not need all the water as flour absorbs different amounts of water depending on its age and the moisture content in the air. It should be just slightly sticky and will firm up as you knead it.

Knead for eight to 10 minutes, or until the dough seems elastic and most of the joints and lines have worked themselves out. Place in a bowl, cover with a damp dish towel, and leave for 30 minutes in a slightly warm area, or at room temperature in the summer.

Divide the dough into 10 equal portions and roll each into golf ball-size balls; cover. Flour your counter and rolling pin. Roll each ball into a 5–6-inch circle. The best way is to keep rolling in one direction, turning the dough a quarter of a circle to get a round shape.

Heat a tava, nonstick skillet, or flat (nonridged) stovetop grill pan until quite hot. Toss the chapati from one hand to the other to remove excess flour, and place on the pan. Reduce the heat to medium and cook until small bubbles appear on the underside, about 10 to 20 seconds, then turn. Cook this side until it has small dark beige spots.

If you have a gas stove, now place the bread directly over a flame using tongs. It will puff immediately. Leave it for 10 seconds until dark spots appear, then turn and cook on the other side for a few seconds, then remove to a plate. If you have an electric cooker, press down gently on the cooked bread over the stove; as you press one area the rest should puff up. Then tackle the next area. This way the bread should puff up all over. Either way, repeat with the rest of the breads, keeping the cooked breads warm, wrapped in foil, in a low oven.

MAKES 10, CAN BE DOUBLED

scant 2¼ cups chapati flour (or half whole wheat and half all-purpose flour), plus more to dust
salt (optional)

These flatbreads are absolutely delicious, flaky, and slightly crisp. They can be plain, cooked with a spice or other flavoring, or even stuffed with a vegetable before cooking. My two favorite types are in the box below right, but you can add anything you like. You can make parathas with vegetable oil, butter, or ghee ... needless to say, the butter and ghee versions have more flavor, but those made with oil are also delicious. Please note that the parathas in the photograph were made using whole wheat chapati flour, but you can use plain white chapati flour if you prefer.

Paratha, many ways

Mix generous ¾–scant 1 cup of water into the flour and knead for eight to 10 minutes, or until the dough seems smooth and elastic and most of the joints and lines have worked themselves out. Make a long log from the dough and divide into 10 balls.

Heat a tava, flat (nonridged) stovetop grill pan, or skillet. Taking one ball of dough at a time, roll out into a 6-inch circle on a floured counter. Brush ¾ teaspoon of oil, ghee, or butter over the surface, sprinkle over a little salt, some flavorings if you want (see below right), and then a fine scattering of flour. Starting with the near edge of the bread, roll away from you into a very tight log (jelly-roll style). Then using your palms, roll this log a bit longer and thinner. Coil the log in on itself in a tight circular motion and pat down into a thick disk. Flour both sides and roll out into a 6–7-inch circle again.

Pat off the excess flour and place the paratha on the hot pan, turning the heat to medium-high. Cook until light brown spots appear on the underside, around 10 to 15 seconds. Turn over and brush ¾ teaspoon of the oil, butter, or ghee over the surface (or do what I do and drizzle it over, then spread with the back of the spoon). Flip the bread again and repeat with more oil. Now, using the edge of the spoon or a knife, make small slashes over the bread to help it crisp up. Turn once again and repeat the slashes. By now the bread should be done, with lovely golden brown spots on both sides. Repeat with the rest and serve hot or at room temperature.

MAKES 10

scant 2¼ cups chapati flour (atta), plus more
  to dust
small bowl of vegetable oil, ghee or melted
  unsalted butter
good pinch of salt

Flavor variations

Spicy: sprinkle a pinch of ajowan seeds and chili powder over each bread with the salt, then flour, roll, and cook as in main recipe.

Mint: sprinkle ¾ teaspoon dried mint (powdered between your fingers) over each bread with the salt, then flour, roll, and cook as in the main recipe.

ON THE
SIDE

A restaurant dish and probably a hybrid of some of India's more popular homegrown potato recipes. I have to say this dish beats my own Punjabi cumin potatoes, and it goes with almost everything.

Best ever Bombay potatoes

Bring a large pot of water to a boil and salt it well. Place in the potatoes and boil until just tender (up to 30 minutes). When cool enough to handle, peel and chop into 1-inch cubes.

Blend together the ginger, garlic, and quartered tomato until smooth.

Heat the oil in a large nonstick skillet. Add the cumin and mustard seeds and, once the cumin starts to darken, add the onion. Cook for a minute before adding the ginger and garlic mixture, the ground spices, and salt. Sauté gently for one to two minutes or until the garlic smells cooked. If you are not sure, taste; it should seem harmonious.

Add the tomato wedges, stir well, and cook for three to four minutes. Tip in the potatoes and cook for three to five minutes to absorb the flavors. Check the seasoning, stir in the chopped cilantro, and serve.

SERVES 4 TO 6

salt, to taste
3 large potatoes (around 2 pounds in total), halved
½-ounce gingerroot, peeled weight
3 garlic cloves, peeled
2 large-ish tomatoes, one quartered, the other cut into slim wedges
4 tablespoons vegetable oil
¾ teaspoon cumin seeds
1 teaspoon mustard seeds
1 large onion, roughly chopped
⅔ teaspoon turmeric
2 teaspoons ground coriander
1 teaspoon ground cumin
1 teaspoon garam masala
½–¾ teaspoon chili powder
large handful of chopped cilantro leaves

Cauliflower, potatoes, and shredded ginger
SERVES 4

A simple dish that is great with a lentil curry. Any leftovers make great panini-like sandwiches, with Tangy Herb Chutney (see page 34).

Heat 4 tablespoons of vegetable oil in a large nonstick pan, karahi or wok. Add 1½ teaspoons of cumin seeds and cook until they are aromatic. Add 2–3 whole, pierced green chiles and ¾–1-ounce of julienned gingerroot and cook until the ginger starts to color. Now add 1 tablespoon of ground coriander, 1 teaspoon of ground cumin, and ¾ teaspoon each of turmeric and garam masala with some salt. Cook for one minute. Tip in 14 ounces of cauliflower florets, 9 ounces of peeled potato wedges, and a 2 tablespoons of water. Stir well to coat. Cover and cook gently over medium heat until the vegetables are cooked (around 15 minutes). Stir in 1½ teaspoons of dried mango powder, or 1 small tomato, chopped, and a handful of chopped cilantro leaves. Taste, adjust the seasoning and spices, then serve.

If you are a fennel fan, this is a great dish. Panch phoran is a blend of five seeds; if you don't have any you can use a roughly even combination of cumin, mustard, fennel, nigella, and fenugreek seeds (though the latter can be left out). This goes well with grilled or tandoori food such as the Tandoori Paneer in my "PLT" (see page 69).

Five-spiced fennel with tomato

Heat the oil in a nonstick pan. Add the panch phoran and chiles; when the seeds stop popping and are aromatic, add the onion. Cook until golden.

Meanwhile, blend together the tomatoes, ginger, and garlic with a stick blender until smooth. Add to the browned onions with all the spices and salt. Cook until completely reduced.

Meanwhile, trim off any leafy fronds from the fennel bulb, chop, and set aside. Remove any tough or browned external leaves and cut the bulb into wedges through the root. Add the fennel to the reduced sauce with a good splash of water and bring to a boil. Cover and cook until the fennel is tender, around five to seven minutes.

Take off the lid and cook off the excess liquid in the pan; the sauce you end up with should be thick. Taste and adjust the seasoning, sprinkle over the fennel fronds, and serve.

SERVES 2, CAN BE DOUBLED

2½ tablespoons vegetable oil
¾ teaspoon panch phoran
1–2 dried red chiles, broken in half
½ onion, sliced
2 large-ish tomatoes
½ ounce gingeroot, peeled weight
2 garlic cloves, peeled
1 teaspoon ground cumin
⅔ teaspoon garam masala
1½ teaspoons ground coriander
salt, to taste
1 large fennel bulb, washed

I eat spinach regularly, it seems to go with so many things and is so quick and easy. You can make this with baby spinach or shredded large leaf spinach and leave the leaf whole or semiblend it, as I do here, which adds a lovely creaminess.

Sautéed spinach, many ways

Heat the oil and butter in a large sauté pan. Add the onion and cook gently until the edges are golden. Add the ginger and garlic and cook until the garlic no longer smells raw, around one minute. Meanwhile, using a stick blender, blend the tomato until smooth. Add the blended tomato, ground coriander and cumin, and salt to the pan and cook down until it becomes quite thick, the color changes and it releases oil back into the pan. Taste; it should seem harmonious. Add the still-wet spinach and let wilt down completely.

At this stage, you can go two ways. The first is simplest: taste and adjust the seasoning, adding the black pepper and garam masala with the additional ingredient, if using (I like corn), and serve. The second way is to remove two-thirds of the mixture, blend it until smooth, then return to the pan. Add the additional ingredient, if using. Taste and adjust the seasoning with the black pepper and garam masala as above. Serve as it is, or with a swirl of light cream.

SERVES 2, CAN BE DOUBLED

1 tablespoon vegetable oil
1 tablespoon unsalted butter
½ large-ish onion, chopped
⅛ ounce gingerroot, peeled weight, grated
2 fat garlic cloves, peeled and grated
1 ripe tomato, quartered
¾ teaspoon ground coriander
½ teaspoon ground cumin
salt, to taste
7 ounces baby spinach, washed well
¼ teaspoon black pepper
⅓ teaspoon garam masala
dash of light cream (optional)

OPTIONAL EXTRAS
1½ handfuls of corn (I use canned)
1 handful of paneer, cubed
1½ handfuls of chickpeas
2 handfuls of sliced mushrooms

Green beans with coconut
SERVES 4

This takes less than 10 minutes to make, and you can use almost any greens: try shaved asparagus or small broccoli florets. You can buy frozen grated coconut in Asian stores, and it's very useful to have in the freezer.

Heat 2 tablespoons of vegetable oil in a large, nonstick skillet. Add 1 teaspoon of mustard seeds and, once they pop, reduce the heat and add 8 curry leaves. Once the popping dies down again, add ½ onion, minced, and cook until soft. Add 2 teaspoons of minced gingerroot and 11 ounces of green beans, trimmed and cut into ½-inch lengths. Season to taste, add a splash of water, and cook over medium-low heat for around five minutes. Stir in 3 tablespoons of grated coconut and 1 teaspoon of lemon juice, taste, adjust the seasoning, and serve.

Inspired by a dish eaten in a friend's house years ago, this was her Hyderabadi mother-in-law's recipe. She served it as part of a meal, but I love it just on its own with crispy naan. Add chickpeas to the spiced oil before tipping it into the yogurt for extra protein, if you want. Pomegranates add a burst of sweet, sour freshness but you can substitute halved baby tomatoes. Lastly, you can griddle the eggplants instead of frying, it will still be lovely.

Crisp eggplants with sweet spiced yogurt and pomegranates

Pour about ½ inch of oil in a large skillet. Add as many eggplant slices as you can get in one layer and cook over medium-high heat until golden on the base, around two to three minutes. Turn the slices and repeat. Place on two pieces of paper towels to drain off the excess oil, then put in a warm oven to keep warm. Repeat with the remaining eggplant. (Alternatively, you can bake the eggplant slices in a preheated oven at 350°F, spread out in one layer on a large baking sheet, but they will not be as crisp.)

For the topping, heat the oil in a small pan. Add the mustard and cumin seeds and, once they start to pop, add the chiles and curry leaves, and cook for another 10 seconds or until cooked through. Pour into the yogurt with the sugar and seasoning.

Place the eggplants on a large serving plate, slightly overlapping in a circular pattern. Spread the yogurt over the central eggplants, leaving a large 3-inch-ish border. Sprinkle with the pomegranate seeds and chopped cilantro and serve immediately.

SERVES 4

FOR THE EGGPLANTS
vegetable oil, to fry
2 small-ish eggplants (11–12 ounces each), sliced into ½-inch thick, long slices
good handful of pomegranate seeds
handful of chopped cilantro leaves

FOR THE YOGURT TOPPING
1 tablespoon vegetable oil
¾ teaspoon mustard seeds
¾ teaspoon cumin seeds
2 dried red chiles
12–14 curry leaves
generous 1 cup Greek yogurt
2 teaspoons superfine sugar, or to taste
salt
freshly ground black pepper

I know many will think life is too short to stuff okra, but this is such an easy recipe and requires very little cooking or chopping. I find I am often drawn to this dish, which I stuff while I am reading something on my computer, or taking a break and watching TV. This is a Gujarati dish, so it is not too spicy and has an element of sweetness.

Coconut–stuffed okra

Mix together all the filling ingredients, adding salt to taste.

Wash the okra and cut a long, deep slit along the length of each okra. Stuff each with as much filling as you can.

Heat the 2 tablespoons of oil in a large nonstick skillet. Add the asafetida and follow five seconds later with the okra. Give the skillet a gentle shake, cover, and cook over medium-low heat until the okra are soft to the tip of a knife, around seven to eight minutes.

Sprinkle over a little sea salt and serve.

SERVES 4

FOR THE FILLING
1 tablespoon sesame seeds
1 tablespoon grated gingerroot
2 teaspoons ground coriander
1 rounded teaspoon ground cumin
¼ teaspoon chili powder (optional)
¾ teaspoon garam masala
6 tablespoons dry unsweetend coconut
2 rounded tablespoons roasted peanuts, coarsely crushed
handful of chopped cilantro leaves and stalks (around 10g)
2 teaspoons superfine sugar
1 tablespoon lemon juice
1 tablespoon vegetable oil
salt, to taste (ideally sea salt)

FOR THE OKRA
9 ounces okra
2 tablespoons vegetable oil
small pinch of asafetida

Not all lentils have to be cooked to a mush or in a curry. In fact, there are plenty of Indian lentil dishes which are just lightly spiced or flavored and have no sauce. This easy stir-fry showcases the texture of these great, large yellow lentils. You just need to soak them well in advance, which will really cut the cooking time. These are delicious and good with both rice and Indian breads.

Stir-fried Bengal gram with coconut

Heat the oil in a large nonstick skillet. Add the seeds, chiles, and curry leaves. Once the seeds have popped and the cumin has darkened, add the onion. Stir-fry for two to three minutes, then add the garlic. Sauté over gentle heat until the garlic starts to take color. Add the turmeric with a small splash of water and cook until the pan is dry.

Drain, add the soaked lentils and salt, and give them a little stir in the pan. Add some hot water from the kettle, bring to a boil, and simmer for five to 15 minutes, or until the lentils are tender but still retain their shape. (How long they take depends both on how long they were soaked and how old the lentils are, but they can cook very quickly.) If they are still hard, add a little more water and cook a little longer.

Once they are done, stir in the lemon juice, taste and adjust the seasoning, add the coconut, and serve.

SERVES 2 TO 3, CAN BE DOUBLED

3 tablespoons vegetable oil
⅔ teaspoon cumin seeds
1 teaspoon mustard seeds
1–2 dried red chiles, broken in half
8–10 curry leaves
½ onion, minced
4 garlic cloves, peeled and minced
⅓ teaspoon turmeric
½ cup Bengal gram (chana dal), washed well and soaked overnight
salt, to taste
1 teaspoon lemon juice
4 tablespoons grated fresh coconut or 2 rounded tablespoons dry unsweetend coconut

Spiced sesame seed beet with yogurt
SERVES 4

A lovely accompaniment to any barbecue, this is creamy and sweet, with both heat and a lovely nuttiness.

Heat 1 teaspoon of vegetable oil in a pan, letting it pool on one side. Add ½ teaspoon each of mustard and cumin seeds and, once the spluttering dies down, add to 11 ounces of cooked, cubed beet in a bowl. Add a pinch of chili powder, 2½ tablespoons of toasted sesame seeds, 2 tablespoons of shredded mint leaves, generous 1 cup of Greek yogurt, a large pinch of superfine sugar, and salt to taste. Mix, adjust the seasoning, and serve.

Cavolo nero, also known as black cabbage, is a much-loved variety of kale from Tuscany. The texture is interesting—less crisp than our familiar cabbages—and the flavor is deeper. I recently rediscovered it at a friend's house. She simply boiled it and, even prepared like that, it stood out. So I bought some and cooked it this way. It has become a staple in my home in the colder months. Buy a head whose leaves are not too large.

Spiced steam-cooked cavolo nero

Prepare the cavolo nero by pulling the leaves off the central core, and cutting out the tough ribs of the outer leaves. The inner, small leaves can be left whole. Wash all the leaves well.

Heat the oil in a large nonstick pan. Add the cumin and mustard seeds with the chiles and cook until the cumin has darkened a little. Add the onion and sauté gently until soft. Add the garlic and cook gently until just starting to color.

Add the cavolo nero and the remaining spices and salt along with a good splash of water and stir to coat well. Cover and steam-cook for four to five minutes, or until the leaves are just soft. Add the tomato and another splash of water if necessary, cover, and cook for another one or two minutes, or until it has softened and released some of its juices. Taste, adjust the seasoning, and serve.

SERVES 2 TO 3, CAN BE DOUBLED

1 head of cavolo nero
2–2½ tablespoons vegetable oil
¾ teaspoon cumin seeds
¾ teaspoon mustard seeds
1–2 dried red chiles, halved
½ onion, minced
5 large garlic cloves, peeled and chopped
1 teaspoon ground coriander
½ teaspoon garam masala
salt, to taste
1 large-ish tomato, finely chopped
good pinch of freshly ground black pepper

Warm Puy lentils
SERVES 2 TO 3

Earthy but vibrant, I eat these all the time.
  Bring 1 cup of Puy lentils to a boil and cook until just tender, 20 to 25 minutes. Drain well. Add 1 tablespoon of extra virgin olive oil, a fistful of minced cilantro, 2½ teaspoons of roasted ground cumin (see page 9), and 2½ tablespoons of lemon juice, season, and serve.

Broccoli is one of my favorite green vegetables and often on the menu in my home, although it is not traditionally used in India. This dish is simple but has lovely punchy flavors. Here I like to use small capers in brine as I like the extra tang, but if you use salted capers, make sure you give them a good rinse.

Spiced broccoli with capers

Bring a pot of water to a boil, add the broccoli, and return to a boil. Cook for three minutes, then drain.

Heat the oil in a large nonstick skillet or sauté pan. Add the panch phoran and chiles and, once they start to color, add the ginger and garlic, reduce the heat, and sauté gently until the garlic is just cooked, around one minute.

Add the broccoli, capers, salt (be careful as the capers are salty), and a very small splash of water and stir until the water evaporates and the broccoli is cooked to your liking. Taste, adjust the seasoning, and serve.

SERVES 3 TO 4

1 pound broccoli, cut into 2-inch florets
2½ tablespoons vegetable oil
1 teaspoon panch phoran
1–2 dried red chiles, broken in half
½ ounce gingerroot, peeled weight, grated
3 large garlic cloves, peeled and grated
3 rounded teaspoons small capers (ideally those in brine), rinsed
salt, to taste

Ultimate kachumber
SERVES 4 TO 5

A chopped salad served with many Indian meals, this is crunchy, fresh, and delicious. It's a case of simply chopping everything finely and mixing it all together. You need 2 large-ish ripe tomatoes, 7 ounces cucumber, 4 radishes, ½ red onion, and a large handful of cilantro leaves. To this chopped mixture, add 1 tablespoon of extra virgin olive oil, 2 tablespoons of lemon juice, salt, freshly ground pepper, 1 teaspoon of roasted ground cumin (see page 9), and 1 tablespoon of good-quality dried mint (or fresh shredded mint, if you prefer). Add 1 small green chile, seeded and minced, if you'd like more heat. Taste, adjust the seasoning, and serve.

DIVINE
DESSERTS

I love dessert and almost need to finish a meal with something sweet. This lovely recipe is inspired by Indian flavors and the country's love of floral notes. It is a soufflé but don't be afraid, it has never failed me and always rises to the occasion with the pomp and gravitas of a presiding maharaja. It might seem like a long recipe of many stages, but it comes together quite easily. I like to eat the dish by making a dent in the middle of the soufflé and pouring in the cream, so every bite is an ethereal mix of cloud-like pomegranate, sweet-sour raspberries, fragrant rose, and rich cream. My ramekins hold ⅔ cup; try to stick to that volume, or the cooking times will be affected.

Pomegranate soufflés with rose and raspberry cream

Start with the soufflés. Whisk 1⅔ tablespoons of the pomegranate juice into the cornstarch. Bring the remaining juice to a boil and reduce to ½ cup; it takes around four minutes and you will need to pour it back into the measuring cup to check (don't worry if it slightly over-reduces).

Add the 2 tablespoons of sugar over the heat and, once it has dissolved, stir the cornstarch mixture once more and tip it in (it will thicken almost immediately). Return to a boil, whisking all the while, then boil for 1 to 1½ minutes. Scrape into a container you can blend in (I use the same measuring cup and my stick blender). Set aside to cool.

Meanwhile, butter the ramekins well and dust with sugar, turning the ramekins so they are well coated and tapping out the excess.

Take scant ½ cup of the berries, mash well, and push through a nylon strainer. Stir into the cream with the sugar and rose water. Fold in the whole raspberries and adjust the sugar and rose water to taste.

Preheat the oven to 350°F. Whisk the egg whites until they reach soft peaks, then sprinkle in the extra 1½ tablespoons sugar and continue whisking until the meringue is glossy and firm.

Blend the pomegranate mixture until smooth once more. Place in a large bowl and whisk in around one-quarter of the egg white mix. Then, using a large spoon, carefully fold in the rest, trying to keep the lightness as you incorporate all the little lumps. Do not overmix. Spoon equally into the ramekins and flatten the tops with a palette knife or other knife. Run the tip of your thumb around the inner rim of the ramekins and place on the middle shelf of the oven.

Bake for eight to nine minutes, or until well-risen and slightly golden on top. Serve immediately with the rose and raspberry cream.

MAKES 4, CAN BE DOUBLED

FOR THE SOUFFLÉS
generous ¾ cup pure pomegranate juice
2 slightly rounded teaspoons cornstarch
2 tablespoons superfine sugar, plus 1½ tablespoons more for the meringue, plus more for the ramekins
soft unsalted butter, for the ramekins
2 egg whites

FOR THE ROSE AND RASPBERRY CREAM
scant 1¼ cups raspberries
½ cup heavy cream
1½ tablespoons superfine sugar, or to taste
2 teaspoons rose water, or to taste

There is an Indian candy, murabba, which is effectively poached fruit or vegetables in a super-sweet syrup, so they are candied and can be stored for months. This dessert, much loved by my father, always seemed to me to be a waste of good produce, as the end result tastes of sugar and not much else. On the other hand, I love fruits being elevated to dessert status, and poaching a pear is a really elegant and easy way of doing so. The ginger here really complements pears, while the pomegranate seeds help create a dramatic plate and add a lovely astringency and fresh burst of flavor.

Ginger-poached pears with pomegranate and poppy seeds

Place 4 cups of water and the sugar in a pan large enough to hold the pears, and bring to a boil, stirring all the time to help the sugar dissolve. Once the sugar has dissolved, add the lime juice and ginger. Peel the pears, then halve, core, and slice each half into three wedges. Slip straight into the water. Bring back to a boil, then reduce the heat and simmer gently until the pears yield completely to the point of a knife and appear to be slightly glazed, 18 to 25 minutes. Using a slotted spoon, remove the pears from the poaching liquor, making sure you leave the ginger in the pot. Set aside the pears. Continue to simmer the liquid for eight to 10 minutes, until it is a light syrup and the ginger looks glazed. Take off the heat; remove and set aside the glazed ginger.

Dry-roast the poppy seeds in a pan (I use a cast-iron one), shaking often for a couple of minutes until aromatic. If using pistachios, dry-roast these until lightly toasted. Whichever you used, remove them from the pan to prevent further cooking.

When ready to serve, pour the pomegranate juice with the 3 tablespoons of extra sugar into a pan and bring to a boil. Simmer until the bubbles have enough viscosity to remain on top of the sauce and it has reduced to a thin syrup (it will continue to thicken off the heat).

Meanwhile, divide the slices of pear between four plates, spooning the glazed ginger over. Add a good dollop of cold crème fraîche and drizzle over a little of the hot pomegranate syrup (you will have some left, which is delicious and versatile and can be used for everything from spooning over yogurt to sweetening black tea).

Sprinkle with a pinch of poppy seeds, scatter over some pomegranate seeds and mint leaves, and serve.

SERVES 4

½ cup superfine sugar, plus 3 rounded tablespoons for the pomegranate syrup
juice of 1 lime
1¼ ounces gingerroot, peeled and coarsely grated
4 firm-but-ripe pears
1 teaspoon poppy seeds (or ¼ cup pistachios, shelled weight)
2½ cups pomegranate juice
crème fraîche, to serve
seeds from ½ pomegranate
8 mint leaves

These vivacious little morsels are a perfect combination of sweet, tangy poached dried apricots, cold heavy cream, and delicate pistachios. A deceptively delicious dessert, it is refreshing and satisfying and great as part of a dessert buffet or canapé party. This isn't an Indian dish, but my mother has been making these my whole life and, as they are so easy and delicious, the recipe needed to be shared. Orange blossom is my addition to the dish; it adds another dimension and reflects the Indian love for floral essences but, if you don't have any, just leave it out.

Mom's apricots with orange blossom and pistachios

Bring 3 cups of water, the sugar, and lemon zest to a boil in a pan, stirring all the time to help the sugar dissolve. Add the apricots and return to a simmer. Now cut a circle of wax paper to fit the pan, dampen it under a faucet, scrunch it up, then flatten it out and place it in the pan so it rests on the surface of the syrup (this circle of wax paper is called a cartouche). Cook gently until soft but not mushy, 20 to 30 minutes, depending on how hard the apricots were (mine took 25 minutes). Once soft, remove with a slotted spoon and place on a plate. Let cool. Continue to simmer the syrup until it is slightly viscous. Add the orange blossom water, if using. Do not add too much at this stage; you can always add a little more later. Pour into a bowl, cover with plastic wrap, and set aside to cool. (You can do this a day in advance.) When completely cold, remove the lemon zest.

Whip the heavy cream until it holds soft peaks. Create pockets in the apricots by splitting them through their middles, using their natural fold as a guide and making sure both sides are still well attached. Pipe or spoon a generous amount of cream onto the bottom layer, then fold over the top. You should have enough cream in the fruit so that it is well visible. Place on a serving platter, drizzle over the orange blossom syrup, and sprinkle generously with the pistachios. Serve.

SERVES 6 TO 8

generous ⅓ cup superfine sugar
1 large pared strip of unwaxed lemon zest
24 dried apricots (I like large Turkish ones)
½–¾ teaspoons orange blossom water,
    or to taste (optional)
⅔ cup heavy cream
good handful of pistachios, roughly chopped

Luscious beet halva
SERVES 4

I had never eaten this before makng my own, but I think it is one of the best things you can do with a beet!

Coarsely grate 2 large, raw beets (wear gloves to keep from staining your hands). Place in a large nonstick pan with 4 cups of milk and cook, stirring occasionally, until the milk has dried off; it will take more than an hour. Add 3 tablespoons of superfine sugar and 4 tablespoons of unsalted butter and cook, stirring, for another 15 to 20 minutes to help the beet caramelize. It will turn a lovely, deep color. Meanwhile, gently heat 1 teaspoon of unsalted butter and fry 3 tablespoons of raisins with a pinch of ground cardamom and a small fistful of cashews until the nuts are lightly golden. Stir into the halva. Taste, adjust the sugar, and serve hot.

This is really luscious, billowy yet textured. The custard only takes about 15 minutes to make, but you can buy a 14-ounce tub of good-quality custard instead (it will have a vanilla flavor, but will be fine). Packages of grated coconut, from the freezer section at Indian and Asian stores, are the best pantry cheat and I highly recommend them. You can use dry unsweetened instead, but it will not have the same texture or taste. If you like pomegranate juice, I would add some in as below; it adds a lovely flavor and also soaks slightly into the sponge but, if you don't have any, it still works really well.

Mango, pomegranate, berry, and coconut trifle

Start with the custard. Place the milk and cream in a large pan and bring to a boil. Meanwhile, whisk the yolks, the 2 tablespoons of sugar, and the cornstarch together in a large bowl until smooth. Slowly pour in the hot cream mixture, whisking all the while so the eggs do not scramble. Pour the whole thing back into the rinsed-out pan and place over gentle heat. Return to just below a boil over very gentle heat, stirring the mixture constantly; this takes me 10 to 12 minutes. Cook for another 30 to 40 seconds, then take off the heat. Stir in the coconut and let cool.

Place the strawberries and three-quarters of the pomegranate seeds in a bowl and add the pomegranate juice, if using. Add sugar to taste and a squeeze of lemon juice, to balance the sweet-sharp flavors. Mash some of the strawberries into the sauce and let macerate.

Meanwhile, prepare the mangoes. Cut the cheeks from the mangoes, peel, then roughly chop. Cut the sides off the seed and see if you can get any unbruised flesh off these as well.

Whip the cream until it is at the soft peak stage.

Cut the cake into ½-inch slices and line the bottom of a glass trifle bowl. Pour over the macerated strawberries and pomegranate with their juices. Spoon the mango evenly over the top. Pour over the custard. Spoon the cream on top, cover with plastic wrap, and chill in the refrigerator until ready to serve, decorated with the reserved pomegranate seeds. You can also use small glasses to make these trifles in individual portions, which look lovely.

SERVES 6

FOR THE COCONUT CUSTARD

generous ¾ cup whole milk
generous ¾ cup heavy cream
4 egg yolks
2 tablespoons superfine sugar, plus 2
    teaspoons, plus more for the strawberries
1⅓ level teaspoons cornstarch
scant 1 cup grated fresh coconut (I use frozen
    and allow it to defrost)

FOR THE REST

scant 1¼ cups strawberries, washed, hulled,
    and roughly chopped
seeds from 2 pomegranates
5 tablespoons pomegranate juice (optional,
    see recipe introduction)
lemon juice, to taste
2 large, or 3 medium, ripe mangoes
1¼ cups heavy cream
10–11 ounces store-bought sponge cake

This dessert is really special, with the creamy reduced milk, sweet-tart caramelized apple, and ricotta. It is simple to make, but you do need to hover around the kitchen as it cooks to ensure the milk does not catch and burn as it reduces. This means stirring the pan, scraping the bottom with a flat-bottomed spatula, every four to five minutes or so. If you are stepping away from the kitchen, either reduce the heat to its lowest or turn it off until you return. If you prefer you can add 3½ ounces of crumbled paneer instead of ricotta. You can make this a day early and chill in the refrigerator overnight.

Caramelized apple and ricotta kheer

Preheat the oven to 375°F. Place the ricotta, slightly spread out in bits, between two layers of wax paper, put it in the oven, and bake for 40 minutes. As it bakes it will dry out and become slightly hard. Put a timer on so as not to forget about the ricotta as you reduce the milk. Once done, remove from the oven and let cool.

Meanwhile, fill a wide, large pan with enough water to come ¼ inch up the sides, and bring to a boil. Then add the milk, return to a boil, and cook over low heat, stirring very often and scraping the bottom of the pan to stop the milk from catching and burning. Cook until reduced by half, it will take 45 to 50 minutes. (See page 169 for more detailed instructions on how to reduce milk.) Add the rice flour, saffron, and cardamom and gently return to a boil while stirring. Cook for another 10 to 15 minutes, still stirring, adding the 2 tablespoons of sugar halfway. The mixture should be one-third of its original volume. Remove from the heat.

Toward the end of the cooking, peel the apples, and grate on the coarse side of a box grater into long strands (I grate them straight into a nonstick pan). Place on the heat and add the butter and the extra 2 teaspoons of sugar. Sauté over moderate heat until the apple has turned a lovely pale gold and is slightly caramelized, around three minutes. Take off the heat.

Once the milk, apples, and ricotta have cooled, mix together, taste, and adjust the sugar if necessary, adding more milk if the kheer seems too thick. I like mine lightly creamy, but everyone likes it slightly differently.

Pour into a serving dish and chill in the refrigerator. Sprinkle with the slivered almonds to serve.

SERVES 6

scant 1 cup ricotta
6⅓ cups whole milk, plus more if needed
1 tablespoon rice flour
pinch of saffron strands
¼ teaspoon ground cardamom
2 tablespoons superfine sugar, plus
    2 teaspoons, or to taste
2 firm, sweet-tart apples (I use Pink Lady)
1 rounded tablespoon unsalted butter
slivered almonds, to decorate

Hot sticky pineapple, crisp pancakes, cold cream, and a hint of spice. Lovely. These are inspired by a very typical Indian dessert pancake, made in the cold months, that is deep-fried, then glazed in a sugar syrup and eaten with sweetened thickened milk. This is my quicker and easier version and works beautifully. Unfortunately the pancakes cannot be made in advance, but they don't take long to cook (the batter can be ready to go) and it all comes together quite quickly.

Sticky caramelized star anise pineapple on crispy pancakes

Place the sugar in a large skillet and let melt and caramelize until golden. Add 4 tablespoons of boiling water; it will bubble and seize but keep stirring and the caramel will melt back in. Add the pineapple and star anise and cook over moderate heat, turning the pineapple in the caramel often and moving around the skillet if there are obvious hot spots. Once the fruit is lightly golden and glazed, which takes four to five minutes, add two small pieces of butter and shake them in. You can add a spoon of hot water at any time if the caramel looks like it is becoming too dark. Keep cooking the pineapple, turning in the sticky caramel, until the rings have a lovely golden color and are well glazed. Set aside. These can be made in advance and reheated when you are ready to eat; I add the extra small piece of butter as I do so.

Make the pancakes. Mix together the flour, sugar, cardamom, salt, and ground almonds. Add the butter and milk and whisk until homogeneous; it should have the consistency of thick cream.

Heat half the ghee in a large nonstick skillet until quite hot and drop around 1½–2 tablespoons of batter in for each pancake. You should be able to make three at a time, each about 4 inches in diameter (help them spread with a spoon). Reduce the heat to medium-low and cook until golden on both sides and slightly darker at the edges, a matter of one or two minutes each side. Lift out with a slotted spatula and place on paper towels to drain excess ghee. Repeat with the second batch.

Place a pancake on each plate and cover with the shards of pineapple. Top with a spoon of crème fraîche and a star anise from the skillet and sprinkle over the toasted coconut. Serve immediately, drizzling with any of the pineappley, caramelly juices from the skillet.

ENOUGH FOR 6, CAN BE DOUBLED

FOR THE PINEAPPLE
3 tablespoons superfine sugar
4 x ½-inch pineapple rings, skin, eyes, and core removed (I sometimes slice these in half, and a bit of imperfection is good here)
6 star anise
2–3 small pieces of unsalted butter
⅔ cup crème fraîche
3 tablespoons dry unsweetened coconut, lightly toasted until golden

FOR THE CRISPY PANCAKES
½ cup all-purpose flour, sifted
generous ¼ cup superfine sugar
1 brown cardamom pod, seeds pounded in a mortar and pestle (or a pinch of ground cardamom)
pinch of salt
2 tablespoons ground almonds
2 heaping tablespoons unsalted butter, melted
scant ½–½ cup whole milk
4 tablespoons ghee or vegetable oil, for frying

Kulfi is India's national ice cream. It is often served with a mass of clear cornstarch noodles doused in rose syrup. You cannot buy those noodles here, but you can buy very fine pre-roasted vermicelli from Indian stores and I think it's better than the original! I have also discovered violet syrup (I get mine, the Présent brand, online); it has all the floral notes of rose but is more delicate and has fast become a staple in my house (my daughter even drizzles it over pancakes). The entire combination is divine: hot delicate vermicelli, cold creamy kulfi, the slight bite of nuts, all rounded off with a lovely finishing note of violets. I often make a double batch of kulfi in two large pans, so I can save some for later.

Cardamom kulfi with violet-laced vermicelli

Bring the milk to a boil in a heavy-bottom pan over moderate heat, stirring often. You need to make sure it doesn't boil over or burn. Stay close to the pan and stir, scraping the bottom so the milk does not catch, stirring the skin that forms on the surface back in and scraping down the sides of the pan; these bits are all an integral part of the kulfi. Simmer over medium heat and reduce until just 2½–scant 3 cups remains; it will have turned a light cream color. The whole thing will take around 1½ to 2 hours over medium heat, so be prepared and make it at a time when you need to be in the kitchen. It's worth the effort, as a kulfi which is not properly reduced will be icy rather than creamy.

Add most of the sugar and all the ground cardamom, return to a boil, and cook for a few minutes more. Add the cream, then taste and adjust the sugar, bearing in mind that as it freezes the sweetness will dull a little. Let cool, then add the pistachios and almonds.

Pour into your molds (I use ⅔-cup ovenproof bowls and cover with plastic wrap). Once the mixture is cold, place in the freezer; they will take around five to six hours to freeze. Stir once or twice as they are freezing, to redistribute the nuts.

About eight minutes before you want to serve, take out the kulfis. Place a pot of water to boil on the stove. Break the vermicelli and drop large strands into the boiling water on the stove, then boil for one minute. Take one out, it should be soft; if it is, drain all the noodles.

Two to three minutes before serving, place the kulfi molds, open side up, in a deep bowl of just-boiled water to help liquify the edges, making sure the water does not get in the molds. Invert the kulfis onto your serving plates and place a moat of vermicelli around them. Drizzle the syrup over the vermicelli, sprinkle over the chia seeds, if using, and the extra nuts. Add some edible flowers if you can find them, and serve.

MAKES 4, CAN BE DOUBLED
(BUT IF YOU DO, USE 2 PANS OR IT WILL TAKE MUCH LONGER)

6⅓ cups whole milk
3–4 tablespoons superfine sugar, to taste (I add the smaller amount)
½ teaspoon ground cardamom, or to taste
6 tablespoons light cream
1 rounded tablespoon pistachios, sliced, plus more to serve
1 rounded tablespoon almonds, sliced, plus more to serve
2¼–3¼ ounces roasted very fine vermicelli (see recipe introduction. I would make extra, but then I think I am greedy here!)
around 2 tablespoons violet syrup
1 tablespoon chia seeds, to serve (optional)
fresh edible violets, to serve (optional)

I was at first very sceptical at how an egg-free cake would taste and, more importantly, how the texture would be. This recipe was given to me by a friend of mine, Divya, about three years ago. I have to say it was a revelation. It has a lovely texture and crumb and the cake is light and rises really well. The orange syrup adds a lovely sour, sticky note and the dates a great chewy texture, propeling this simple cake into an elegant, impressive dessert. The cakes can be made a day in advance, they won't be hot but they will still be delicious. You can also make one large cake; just make sure it is cooked all the way through by testing with a toothpick.

Fluffy egg-free pistachio cakes with orange syrup and dates

Preheat the oven to 375°F. Line the bottom of eight ⅔–generous ⅔-cup ovenproof molds (mine are metal) with wax paper and butter the sides well.

Beat together the condensed milk and butter until well blended and creamy. Stir in generous 1 cup of water, add all the remaining ingredients, and stir well to mix.

Spoon evenly into the molds; the mixture will be thick. Place in the middle of the oven and bake for 25 minutes, or until a toothpick inserted into the middle comes out clean.

Meanwhile, pour the orange juice and zest and the sugar into a small pan and bring to a boil. Simmer until, when you drop a bit on a cold plate, it feels slightly syrupy to the touch. It will continue to thicken further as it cools.

Place a cake on a plate and spoon over some orange syrup. Place the date slices on the syrup and spoon a generous dollop of the crème fraîche on the side, or on top. Scatter over a few pistachios and serve.

MAKES 8

FOR THE CAKE
scant ⅔ cup unsalted butter, at room
    temperature, plus more for the molds
scant 1⅔–1⅔ cups condensed milk
1 cup pistachios, ground to a coarse powder
scant 2 cups all-purpose flour, sifted
1 teaspoon baking powder
1 teaspoon baking soda
pinch of salt

TO FINISH
juice of 2 large organic oranges and finely
    grated zest of 1
6 tablespoons superfine sugar
8 large unsweetened dates, sliced
crème fraîche, to serve
handful of chopped pistachios, to serve

ACKNOWLEDGMENTS

The first vegetarian influence in my life was my mother, and her simple but delicious take on vegetables cast a positive glow on vegetarian food in my early years. But a proper induction came with the large, extended Jain/vegetarian family into which I married. It was really a case of you marry me, you marry my family, and all that comes with it! In particular I'd like to thank my mother-in-law who, from the very beginning, has openly and passionately shared her knowledge of Indian vegetarian dishes and made sure, throughout the last decade or so, that I try as many delicacies and interesting flavor combinations as she has. Some people say that vegetarians know little about good food; nothing could be further from the truth. My new family are veggie food snobs and seek and expect the best flavors from every meal.

A massive thanks to Heather Holden-Brown and Elly James for their honest and sound guidance; Anne Furniss for green-lighting this book and for her continued support; the team at Quadrille for the much necessary behind-the-scenes work; Lucy Bannell for being as "geeky" about words as I am about food; Claire Peters, Emma Lee, Joss Herd, and Tabatha Hawkins for making the food and book come to glorious, colorful, and appetizing life.

I would also like to thank my family for their continued support as I juggle work and children and, lastly, thank you Shaila for taking the time, as always, to be my sounding board, and whose critical eye and frank comments I have come to rely upon to make sure the book is as good as it can be.

EDITORIAL DIRECTOR Anne Furniss
CREATIVE DIRECTOR Helen Lewis
PROJECT EDITOR Lucy Bannell
DESIGNER Claire Peters
PHOTOGRAPHER Emma Lee

FOOD STYLIST Joss Herd
PROPS STYLIST Tabitha Hawkins
HAIR & MAKE-UP Madge Foster
PRODUCTION DIRECTOR Vincent Smith
PRODUCTION CONTROLLER James Finan

STERLING EPICURE
New York

An Imprint of Sterling Publishing
387 Park Avenue South
New York, NY 10016

First published in 2012 by Quadrille Publishing Limited
www.quadrille.co.uk

First published in North America in 2013 by Sterling Publishing Co., Inc.

ISBN 978-1-4549-0866-1

Distributed in Canada by Sterling Publishing
c/o Canadian Manda Group, 165 Dufferin Street
Toronto, Ontario, Canada M6K 3H6

For information about custom editions, special sales, and premium and corporate purchases, please contact Sterling Special Sales at 800-805-5489 or specialsales@sterlingpublishing.com.

Manufactured in China

2 4 6 8 10 9 7 5 3 1

www.sterlingpublishing.com